Anthem: The Graphic Novel
Mankind has entered a new **Dark Age** in this dystopian future imagined by **Ayn Rand**. The stark horror of a civilization destroyed by envy remains as relevant and arresting today as it did eight decades ago, when ***Anthem*** was first published.

The short novella encapsulated ideas **Rand** had presented earlier in ***We the Living***, and would develop in her epic dramas, ***The Fountainhead*** and ***Atlas Shrugged***. But for millions of readers, ***Anthem*** retains almost mythic appeal.

In this adaptation, award-winning artist **Dan Parsons** teams up with **Jennifer Grossman** of **The Atlas Society** to introduce the story to a new generation with a provocative, graphic presentation that captures the imagination and invites readers on a journey of self-discovery.

AYN RAND'S
ANTHEM
THE GRAPHIC NOVEL

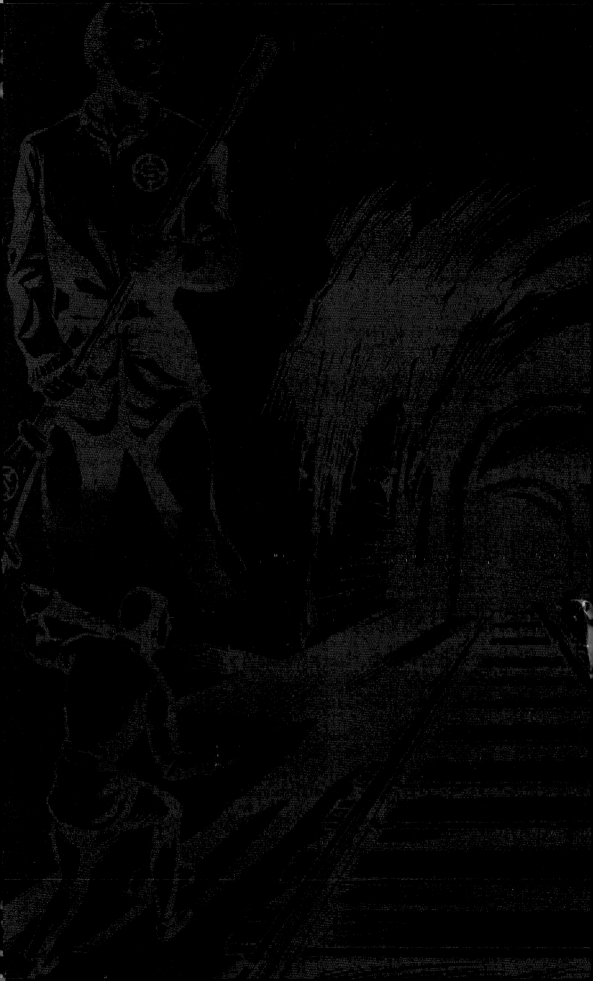

IT IS A SIN TO WRITE THIS...
...IT IS A SIN TO THINK WORDS NO OTHERS THINK AND TO PUT THEM DOWN UPON A PAPER NO OTHERS ARE TO SEE...
IT IS BASE AND EVIL.
IT WAS AS IF WE WERE SPEAKING ALONE TO NO EARS BUT OUR OWN. AND WE KNOW THAT THERE IS NO TRANSGRESSION BLACKER THAN TO DO OR THINK ALONE...
WE HAVE BROKEN THE LAWS
THE LAWS SAY THAT MEN MAY NOT WRITE UNLESS THE COUNCIL OF VOCATIONS BIDS THEM SO...
MAY WE BE FORGIVEN!
BUT THIS IS NOT THE ONLY SIN UPON US....
WE HAVE COMMITED A GREATER CRIME AND FOR THIS THERE IS NO NAME.
WHAT PUNISHMENT AWAITS US IF IT BE DISCOVERED WE KNOW NOT... FOR NO SUCH CRIME HAS COME IN THE MEMORY OF MEN AND THERE ARE NO LAWS TO PROVIDE FOR IT...
THE LAWS SAY THAT NONE AMONG MEN MAY BE ALONE EVER AND AT ANY TIME, FOR THIS IS THE GREAT TRANSGRESSION AND THE ROOT OF ALL EVIL.
BUT WE HAVE BROKEN MANY LAWS...
...WE STOLE THE CANDLES FROM THE LARDER OF THE HOME OF THE STREET SWEEPERS. WE SHALL BE SENTENCED TO TEN YEARS IN THE PALACE OF CORRECTIVE DETENTION IF IT BE DISCOVERED...
...BUT THIS MATTERS NOT.
IT MATTERS ONLY THAT THE LIGHT IS PRECIOUS AND WE SHOULD NOT WASTE IT TO WRITE WHEN WE NEED IT FOR THAT WORK THAT IS OUR CRIME.
NOTHING MATTERS SAVE THE WORK, OUR SECRET, OUR EVIL, OUR PRECIOUS WORK. STILL, WE MUST ALSO WRITE, FOR --MAY THE COUNCIL HAVE MERCY UPON US! --WE WISH TO SPEAK FOR ONCE TO NO EARS BUT OUR OWN...

... OUR NAME IS EQUALITY 7-2521
EQUALITY 7-2521
AS IT WRITTEN ON THE BRACELET THAT ALL MEN WEAR ON THEIR LEFT WRIST.
WE ARE 21 YEARS OLD. WE ARE SIX FEET TALL. THIS IS A BURDEN... FOR THERE ARE NOT MANY MEN WHO ARE SIX FEET TALL...
THERE IS EVIL IN YOUR BONES EQUALITY 7-2521
...YOUR BODY HAS GROWN BEYOND THE BODIES OF YOUR BROTHERS!
WE WERE BORN WITH A CURSE. IT HAS ALWAYS DRIVEN US TO THOUGHTS WHICH ARE FORBIDDEN. WE KNOW THAT WE ARE EVIL.
WE ARE ONE IN ALL AND ALL IN ONE THERE ARE NO MEN ONLY THE GREAT WE ONE INDIVISIBLE AND FOREVER
WE STRIVE TO BE LIKE OUR BROTHER MEN...FOR ALL MEN MUST BE ALIKE.
THESE WORDS ARE TRUE FOR THEY ARE WRITTEN ON THE PALACE OF THE WORLD COUNCIL. THUS IT HAS BEEN SINCE THE GREAT REBIRTH AND FURTHER BACK THAN NO MAN CAN KNOW.
BUT WE MUST NEVER SPEAK OF THE TIMES BEFORE THE GREAT REBIRTH, ELSE WE ARE SENTENCED TO THREE YEARS IN THE PALACE OF CORRECTIVE DETENTION....
IT IS ONLY THE OLD ONES WHO WHISPER ABOUT IT IN THE EVENINGS IN THE HOME OF THE USELESS.
THEY WHISPER MANY STRANGE THINGS, OF THE TOWERS WHICH ROSE TO THE SKY IN THOSE UNMENTIONABLE TIMES AND OF LIGHTS WHICH BURNED WITHOUT FLAME...
BUT THOSE TIMES WERE EVIL. AND THOSE TIMES PASSED AWAY...
MEN SAW THE GREAT TRUTH : ALL MEN ARE ONE AND THERE IS NO WILL SAVE THE WILL OF ALL MEN TOGETHER...

ALL MEN ARE GOOD AND WISE. IT IS ONLY WE, EQUALITY 7-2521. WE ALONE WERE BORN WITH A CURSE.... WE ARE NOT LIKE OUR BROTHERS... AND AS WE LOOK BACK ON OUR LIFE WE SEE IT HAS EVER BEEN THUS AND THAT IT HAS BROUGHT US TO OUR LAST GREAT TRANSGRESSION. OUR CRIME OF CRIMES HIDDEN UNDER THE GROUND.
WE REMEMBER THE HOME OF THE INFANTS WHERE WE LIVED TILL WE WERE FIVE YEARS OLD TOGETHER WITH ALL OF THE OTHER CHILDREN WHO HAD BEEN BORN IN THE SAME YEAR...
WE WERE JUST LIKE ALL OUR BROTHERS THEN...
SAVE FOR ONE TRANSGRESSION...
WE FOUGHT WITH OUR BROTHERS
THERE ARE FEW OFFENCES BLACKER THAN TO FIGHT WITH OUR BROTHERS AT ANY AGE FOR ANY CAUSE WHATSOEVER...THE COUNCIL OF HOME TOLD US SO...
...AND OF ALL THE CHILDREN THAT YEAR WE WERE LOCKED IN THE CELLAR MOST OFTEN...
...WHEN WE WERE FIVE YEARS OLD WE WERE SENT TO THE HOME OF THE STUDENTS WHERE THERE ARE TEN WARDS FOR TEN YEARS OF LEARNING. MEN MUST LEARN TILL THEY REACH THEIR FIFTEENTH YEAR THEN THEY GO TO WORK. IN THE HOME OF THE STUDENTS WE ROSE WHEN THE BIG BELL RANG IN THE TOWER AND WENT TO OUR BEDS WHEN THE GREAT BELL RANG AGAIN...

BEFORE WE REMOVED OUR GARMENTS WE STOOD IN THE GREAT SLEEPING HALL AND SAID WITH THE TEACHERS...
WE ARE NOTHING. MANKIND IS ALL. BY THE GRACE OF OUR BROTHERS WE ARE ALLOWED OUR LIVES... WE EXIST THROUGH, BY AND FOR OUR BROTHERS WHO ARE THE STATE...AMEN!

WE, EQUALITY 7-2521 WERE NOT HAPPY IN THOSE YEARS IN THE HOME OF THE STUDENTS...
IT WAS NOT THAT THE LEARNING WAS TOO HARD. IT WAS THAT IT WAS TOO EASY...
IT IS NOT GOOD TO BE DIFFERENT FROM OUR BROTHERS. BUT IT IS EVIL TO BE SUPERIOR TO THEM.

WE LOOKED UPON UNION 5-3992 WHO WERE A PALE BOY WITH ONLY HALF A BRAIN AND WE TRIED TO SAY AND DO AS THEY DID THAT WE MIGHT BE LIKE THEM... LIKE UNION 5-3992
BUT SOMEHOW THE TEACHERS KNEW THAT WE WERE NOT.
THE TEACHERS WERE JUST FOR THEY HAD BEEN APPOINTED BY THE COUNCILS, AND THE COUNCILS ARE THE VOICE OF ALL JUSTICE. FOR THEY ARE THE VOICE OF ALL MEN.
AND IF SOMETIMES IN THE SECRET DARKNESS OF OUR HEART WE REGRET THAT WHICH BEFELL US ON OUR FIFTEENTH BIRTHDAY WE KNOW THAT IT WAS THROUGH OUR OWN GUILT...
WE HAD BROKEN THE LAW FOR WE HAD NOT PAID HEED TO THE WORDS OF THE TEACHERS...THE TEACHERS SAID TO US ALL:
DARE NOT CHOOSE IN YOUR MINDS THE WORK YOU WOULD LIKE TO DO WHEN YOU LEAVE THE HOME OF THE STUDENTS. YOU SHALL DO WHAT THE COUNCIL OF VOCATIONS KNOWS IN ITS GREAT WISDOM WHERE YOU ARE NEEDED BY YOUR BROTHER MEN, BETTER THAN YOU CAN KNOW IT IN YOUR UNWORTHY LITTLE MINDS. AND IF YOU ARE NOT NEEDED BY YOUR BROTHER MEN THERE IS NO REASON FOR YOU TO BURDEN THE EARTH WITH YOUR BODIES.
WE KNEW THIS WELL IN THE YEARS OF OUR CHILDHOOD BUT OUR OLD CURSE BROKE OUR WILL. WE WERE GUILTY AND CONFESS IT HERE...
WE WERE GUILTY OF THE GREAT TRANSGRESSION OF PREFERENCE...
WE PREFERRED SOME WORK AND SOME LESSONS TO OTHERS...
WE LOVED THE SCIENCE OF THINGS. WE WISHED TO KNOW ABOUT ALL THINGS WHICH MAKE THE EARTH AROUND US. WE THINK THAT THERE ARE MYSTERIES IN THE SKY AND THE WATER...
WE LEARNED FROM OUR TEACHERS THAT THE EARTH IS FLAT AND THAT THE SUN REVOLVES AROUND IT WHICH CAUSES THE DAY AND THE NIGHT...
...WE LEARNED HOW TO BLEED MEN TO CURE THEM OF ALL AILMENTS.

WE LOVED THE SCIENCE OF THINGS...
AND IN THE SECRET HOUR, WHEN WE AWOKE AND THERE WERE NO BROTHERS AROUND US, BUT ONLY THEIR SHAPES IN THE BEDS AND THEIR SNORES, WE CLOSED OUR EYES, HELD OUR LIPS SHUT, STOPPED OUR BREATH THAT NO SHUDDER MIGHT LET OUR BROTHERS GUESS THAT WE WISHED THAT WE WOULD BE SENT TO THE HOME OF THE SCHOLARS.
ALL OF THE GREAT MODERN INVENTIONS COME FROM THE HOME OF THE SCHOLARS SUCH AS THE NEWEST ONE...WHICH WAS FOUND ONLY A HUNDRED YEARS AGO...HOW TO MAKE CANDLES FROM WAX AND STRING.
AND ALSO HOW TO MAKE GLASS...WHICH IS PUT IN OUR WINDOWS TO PROTECT US FROM THE RAIN.
TO FIND THESE THINGS THE SCHOLARS MUST STUDY THE EARTH AND LEARN FROM THE SANDS AND THE WINDS AND THE ROCKS...
IF WE WENT TO THE HOME OF THE SCHOLARS WE COULD LEARN FROM THESE ALSO. WE COULD ASK QUESTIONS OF THESE, FOR THEY DO NOT FORBID QUESTIONS. QUESTIONS GIVE US NO REST. WE MUST KNOW THAT WE MAY KNOW.
SO WE WISHED TO BE SENT TO THE HOME THE OF SCHOLARS. WE WISHED IT SO MUCH THAT OUR HANDS TREMBLED UNDER THE BLANKETS AND WE BIT OUR ARM TO STOP THAT OTHER PAIN THAT WE COULD NOT ENDURE...IT WAS EVIL AND WE DARED NOT FACE OUR BROTHERS IN THE MORNING.
AND WE WERE PUNISHED WHEN THE COUNCIL OF VOCATIONS CAME TO GIVE US OUR LIFE MANDATES WHICH TELL THOSE WHO REACH THEIR FIFTEENTH BIRTHDAY WHAT THEIR WORK WILL BE FOR THE REST OF THEIR DAYS...
JUSTICE 7-2724
CARPENTER.
THE COUNCIL OF VOCATIONS CAME THE FIRST OF SPRING...
THE WILL OF OUR BROTHERS BE DONE!
WE WHO WERE FIFTEEN AND ALL THE TEACHERS CAME INTO THE GREAT HALL...

SO WE WAITED IN THE GREAT HALL AND THEN WE HEARD THE COUNCIL OF VOCATIONS CALL OUR NAME...
EQUALITY 7-2521
THEY SEEMED OLDER THAN THE MARBLE OF THE TEMPLE OF THE WORLD COUNCIL, THEY SAT BEFORE US AND DID NOT MOVE...
BUT WE KNEW THAT THEY WERE ALIVE FOR A FINGER OF THE OLDEST ROSE POINTED TO US AND FELL DOWN AGAIN. THIS WAS THE ONLY THING WHICH MOVED. THE LIPS OF THE ELDEST DID NOT MOVE AS THEY SAID
STREET SWEEPER
WE FELT THE CORDS OF OUR NECK GROW TIGHT AS OUR HEAD ROSE: WE WERE HAPPY.
WE KNEW WE HAD BEEN GUILTY BUT NOW WE HAD A WAY TO ATONE FOR IT...
WE WOULD ACCEPT OUR LIFE MANDATE. WE WOULD WORK FOR OUR BROTHERS. WE WOULD ERASE OUR SIN AGAINST THEM. WE WERE PROUD.
THE WILL OF OUR BROTHERS BE DONE.
...AND WE LOOKED STRAIGHT INTO THE EYES OF THE COUNCIL, BUT THEIR EYES WERE AS COLD BLUE GLASS BUTTONS.
SO WE WENT TO THE HOME OF THE STREET SWEEPERS
THERE IS A SUNDIAL IN ITS COURTYARD BY WHICH THE COUNCIL OF THE HOME CAN TELL THE HOUR OF THE DAY AND WHEN TO RING THE BELL.
WHEN THE BELL RINGS WE ARISE FROM OUR BEDS...
THE SUNDIAL MARKS OFF A HALF HOUR WHILE WE DRESS AND EAT OUR BREAKFAST...
THEN WE GO TO WORK IN THE STREETS OF THE CITY...
WHEN THE SUN IS HIGH WE RETURN TO THE HOME FOR OUR MIDDAY MEAL... ONE HALF HOUR IS ALLOWED. THEN WE GO TO WORK AGAIN.
WHEN THE SHADOW IS BLUE ON THE PAVEMENTS WE COME BACK TO HAVE DINNER, ONE HOUR IS ALLOWED.

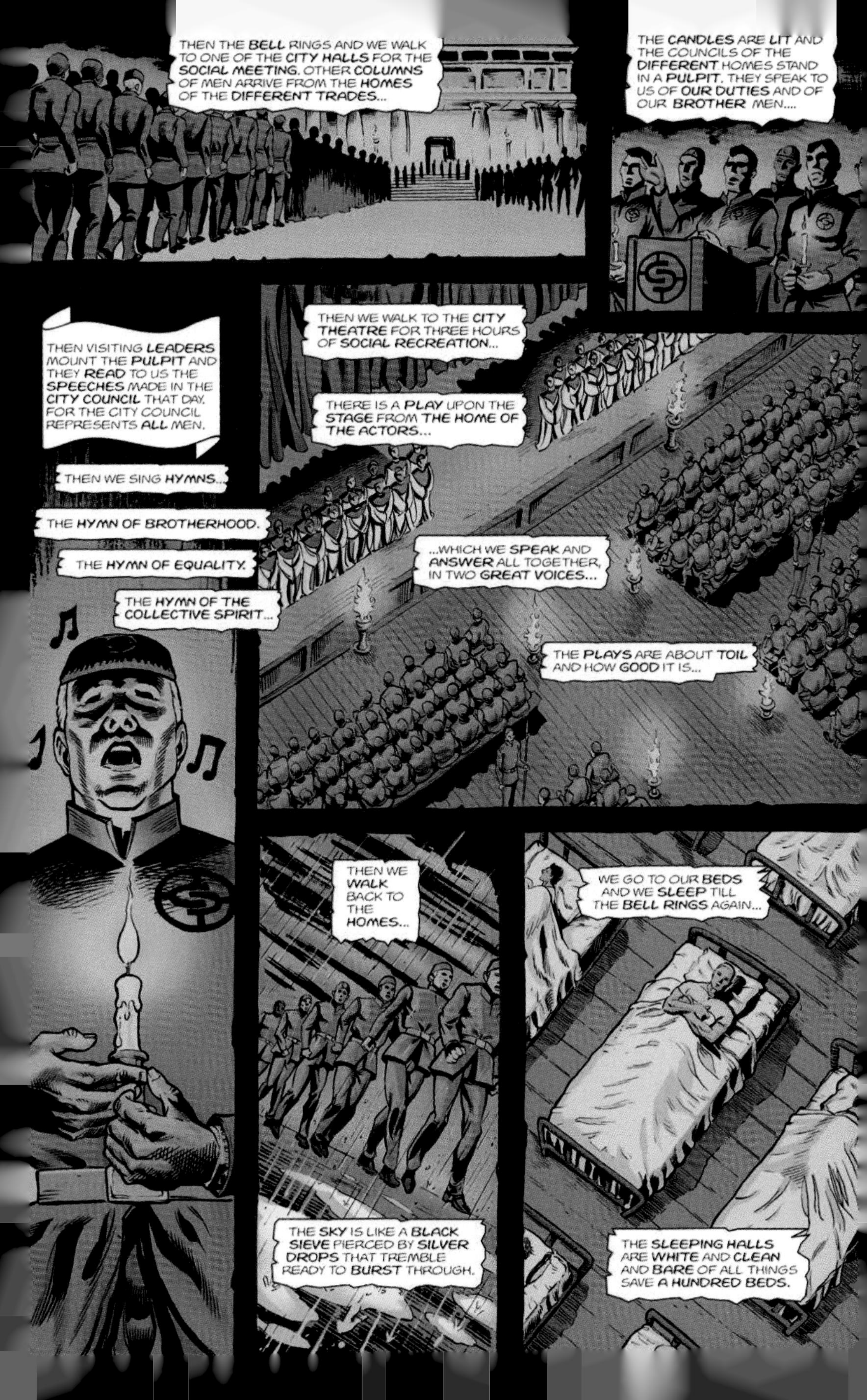
THEN THE BELL RINGS AND WE WALK TO ONE OF THE CITY HALLS FOR THE SOCIAL MEETING. OTHER COLUMNS OF MEN ARRIVE FROM THE HOMES OF THE DIFFERENT TRADES...
THE CANDLES ARE LIT AND THE COUNCILS OF THE DIFFERENT HOMES STAND IN A PULPIT. THEY SPEAK TO US OF OUR DUTIES AND OF OUR BROTHER MEN....
THEN VISITING LEADERS MOUNT THE PULPIT AND THEY READ TO US THE SPEECHES MADE IN THE CITY COUNCIL THAT DAY, FOR THE CITY COUNCIL REPRESENTS ALL MEN.
THEN WE SING HYMNS...
THE HYMN OF BROTHERHOOD.
THE HYMN OF EQUALITY.
THE HYMN OF THE COLLECTIVE SPIRIT...
THEN WE WALK TO THE CITY THEATRE FOR THREE HOURS OF SOCIAL RECREATION...
THERE IS A PLAY UPON THE STAGE FROM THE HOME OF THE ACTORS...
...WHICH WE SPEAK AND ANSWER ALL TOGETHER, IN TWO GREAT VOICES...
THE PLAYS ARE ABOUT TOIL AND HOW GOOD IT IS...
THEN WE WALK BACK TO THE HOMES...
THE SKY IS LIKE A BLACK SIEVE PIERCED BY SILVER DROPS THAT TREMBLE READY TO BURST THROUGH.
WE GO TO OUR BEDS AND WE SLEEP TILL THE BELL RINGS AGAIN...
THE SLEEPING HALLS ARE WHITE AND CLEAN AND BARE OF ALL THINGS SAVE A HUNDRED BEDS.

THUS WE HAVE LIVED EACH DAY OF FOUR YEARS UNTIL TWO SPRINGS AGO WHEN OUR CRIME HAPPENED. THUS MUST ALL MEN LIVE UNTIL THEY ARE FORTY. AT FORTY THEY ARE WORN OUT. AT FORTY THEY ARE SENT TO THE HOME OF THE USELESS WHERE THE OLD ONES LIVE.
THE OLD ONES DO NOT WORK. THE STATE TAKES CARE OF THEM. THEY SIT IN THE SUN IN THE SUMMER AND THEY SIT BY THE FIRE IN THE WINTER...
THEY DO NOT SPEAK FOR THEY ARE WEARY. THE OLD ONES KNOW THAT THEY ARE SOON TO DIE. WHEN A MIRACLE HAPPENS AND SOME LIVE TO BE FORTY FIVE THEY ARE THE ANCIENT ONES.
SUCH IS TO BE OUR LIFE AND THAT OF ALL OUR BROTHERS AND OF THE BROTHERS WHO CAME BEFORE US.
SUCH WOULD HAVE BEEN OUR LIFE HAD WE NOT COMMITTED OUR CRIME WHICH CHANGED ALL THINGS FOR US.
WE HAD BEEN A GOOD STREET SWEEPER SAVE FOR OUR CURSED WISH TO KNOW. WE LOOKED TOO LONG AT THE STARS AT NIGHT AND AT THE TREES AND AT THE EARTH...
AND WHEN WE CLEANED THE HOME OF THE SCHOLARS WE GATHERED THE GLASS VIALS, THE PIECES OF METAL, THE DRIED BONES WHICH THEY HAD DISCARDED.
WE WISHED TO KEEP THESE THINGS AND TO STUDY THEM...
SO WE CARRIED THEM TO THE CITY CESSPOOL.
AND THEN WE MADE THE DISCOVERY...
IT WAS ON THE SPRING BEFORE LAST...
WE WERE WITH UNION 5-3992, THEY OF THE HALF BRAIN AND WITH INTERNATIONAL 4-8818. UNION 5-3992 ARE A SICKLY LAD AND SOMETIMES STRICKEN WITH CONVULSIONS BUT INTERNATIONAL 4-8818 ARE DIFFERENT.
WE CANNOT LOOK UPON INTERNATIONAL 4-8818 AND NOT SMILE. FOR THEY WERE NOT LIKED IN THE HOME OF THE STUDENTS. AND THEY WERE ALSO NOT LIKED BECAUSE THEY TOOK PIECES OF COAL AND DREW PICTURES ON THE WALL...
THEY WERE PICTURES THAT MADE MEN LAUGH. BUT ONLY OUR BROTHERS IN THE HOME OF THE ARTISTS ARE PERMITTED TO DRAW PICTURES...
SO INTERNATIONAL 4-8818 WERE SENT TO THE HOME OF THE STREET SWEEPERS LIKE OURSELVES.

INTERNATIONAL 4-8818 AND WE ARE FRIENDS. THIS IS AN EVIL THING TO SAY, FOR ITS A GREAT TRANSGRESSION, THE GREAT TRANSGRESSION OF PREFERENCE...TO LOVE ANY AMONG MEN BETTER THAN THE OTHERS--SINCE WE MUST LOVE ALL MEN, AND ALL MEN ARE OUR FRIENDS...
SO INTERNATIONAL 4-8818 AND WE HAVE NEVER SPOKEN OF IT. BUT WE KNOW. WE BOTH KNOW OTHER THINGS ALSO, STRANGE WORDLESS THINGS THAT FRIGHTEN US...
SO ON THAT DAY OF SPRING BEFORE LAST, UNION 5-3992 WERE STRICKEN WITH CONVULSION ON THE EDGE OF THE CITY...NEAR THE CITY THEATRE...
WE LEFT THEM TO LIE IN THE SHADE OF THE THEATRE TENT AND WE WENT WITH INTERNATIONAL 4-8818 TO FINISH OUR WORK...
WE CAME TOGETHER TO THE GREAT RAVINE BEHIND THE THEATRE...
BEYOND THE RAVINE THERE IS A PLAIN AND BEYOND THE PLAIN THERE LIES THE UNCHARTED FOREST...
...ABOUT WHICH WE MUST NOT THINK.
WE WERE TO GATHER THE PAPER AND RAGS WHICH THE WIND HAD BLOWN FROM THE THEATRE.
WE SAW AN IRON BAR AMONG THE WEEDS... IT WAS OLD AND RUSTED FROM MANY RAINS...
WE COULD NOT MOVE IT, SO WE CALLED INTERNATIONAL 4-8818.
WE SCRAPED THE EARTH AROUND THE BAR ... ALL OF A SUDDEN THE EARTH FELL IN BEFORE US!
INTERNATIONAL 4-8818 STEPPED BACK... BUT WE PULLED AT THE GRILL AND IT GAVE WAY!

WE SHALL GO DOWN!
IT IS FORBIDDEN.
THE COUNCIL DOES NOT KNOW OF THIS HOLE, SO IT CANNOT BE FORBIDDEN.
SINCE THE COUNCIL DOES NOT KNOW OF THIS HOLE, THERE CAN BE NO LAW PERMITTING TO ENTER IT. AND EVERYTHING THAT IS NOT PERMITTED IS FORBIDDEN!
WE SHALL GO NONE THE LESS!
THEY WERE FRIGHTENED, BUT THEY STOOD AND WATCHED US GO.
WE COULD SEE NOTHING BELOW US.
AND ABOVE US... THE HOLE OPEN UPON THE SKY GREW SMALLER AND SMALLER... TIL IT CAME TO THE SIZE OF A BUTTON...
BUT STILL WE WENT DOWN...
THEN OUR FOOT TOUCHED THE GROUND.
WE RUBBED OUR EYES, FOR WE COULD NOT SEE.
THEN OUR EYES BECAME USED TO THE DARKNESS, BUT WE COULD NOT BELIEVE WHAT WE SAW...

NO MEN KNOWN TO US COULD HAVE BUILT THIS PLACE, NOR THE MEN KNOWN TO OUR BROTHERS WHO LIVED BEFORE US. AND YET IT WAS BUILT BY MEN...
ITS WALLS WERE HARD AND SMOOTH TO THE TOUCH. IT FELT LIKE STONE, BUT IT WAS NOT STONE.
WE KNELT, AND WE CRAWLED FORWARD, OUR HAND GROPING ALONG THE IRON LINE TO SEE WHERE IT WOULD LEAD.
BUT THERE WAS AN UNBROKEN NIGHT AHEAD. ONLY THE IRON TRACKS GLOWED THROUGH IT, STRAIGHT AND WHITE, CALLING US TO FOLLOW.
BUT WE COULD NOT FOLLOW, FOR WE WERE LOSING THE PUDDLE OF LIGHT BEHIND US. SO WE TURNED AND WE CRAWLED BACK, OUR HAND ON THE IRON LINE, AND OUR HEART BEAT IN OUR FINGERTIPS, WITHOUT REASON. AND THEN WE KNEW.
WE KNEW SUDDENLY, THAT THIS PLACE WAS LEFT FROM THE UNMENTIONABLE TIMES. SO IT WAS TRUE! THOSE TIMES HAD BEEN!.. AND ALL THE WONDERS OF THOSE TIMES. HUNDREDS UPON HUNDREDS OF YEARS AGO MEN KNEW SECRETS WHICH WE HAVE LOST. AND WE THOUGHT: "THIS IS A FOUL PLACE. THEY ARE DAMNED WHO TOUCH THE THINGS OF THE UNMENTIONABLE TIMES." BUT OUR HAND WHICH FOLLOWED THE TRACK, AS WE CRAWLED, CLUNG TO THE IRON AS IF IT WOULD NOT LEAVE IT, AS IF THE SKIN OF OUR HAND WERE THIRSTY AND BEGGING OF THE METAL... SOME SECRET FLUID BEATING IN ITS COLDNESS.
WE RETURNED TO THE EARTH. INTERNATIONAL 4-8818 LOOKED UPON US AND STEPPED BACK.
EQUALITY 7-2521, YOUR FACE IS WHITE.

WE SHALL REPORT OUR FIND TO THE CITY COUNCIL AND BOTH OF US WILL BE REWARDED.
WE SHALL NOT REPORT OUR FIND TO THE CITY COUNCIL. WE SHALL NOT REPORT IT TO ANY MEN.
THEY RAISED THEIR HANDS TO THEIR EARS...FOR THEY HAD NEVER HEARD SUCH WORDS AS THESE...
INTERNATIONAL 4-8818, WILL YOU REPORT US TO THE COUNCIL AND SEE US LASHED TO DEATH BEFORE YOUR EYES?
RATHER WOULD WE DIE.
THEN, KEEP SILENT. THIS PLACE IS OURS. THIS PLACE BELONGS TO US, EQUALITY 7-2521 AND NO OTHER MEN ON EARTH.
AND IF EVER WE SURRENDER IT, WE SHALL SURRENDER OUR LIFE WITH IT ALSO.
THE WILL OF THE COUNCIL IS ABOVE ALL THINGS, FOR IT IS THE WILL OF OUR BROTHERS, WHICH IS HOLY. BUT IF YOU WISH IT SO, WE SHALL OBEY YOU. RATHER SHALL WE BE EVIL WITH YOU, THAN GOOD WITH ALL OUR BROTHERS. MAY THE COUNCIL HAVE MERCY UPON BOTH OUR HEARTS!
THEN WE WALKED AWAY TOGETHER AND BACK TO THE HOME OF THE STREET SWEEPERS.
AND WE WALKED IN SILENCE.

THUS DID IT COME TO PASS EACH NIGHT, WHEN THE STARS ARE HIGH AND THE STREET SWEEPERS SIT IN THE CITY THEATRE, WE STEAL OUT AND RUN THROUGH THE DARKNESS TO OUR PLACE.
IT IS EASY TO LEAVE THE THEATRE WHEN THE CANDLES ARE BLOWN AND THE ACTORS COME ONTO THE STAGE.
LATER, IT IS EASY TO STEAL THROUGH THE SHADOWS AND FALL IN LINE NEXT TO INTERNATIONAL 4-8818 AS THE COLUMN LEAVES THE THEATRE...
IT IS DARK IN THE STREETS AND THERE ARE NO MEN ABOUT, FOR NO MEN MAY WALK THROUGH THE CITY WHEN THEY HAVE NO MISSION TO WALK THERE.
EACH NIGHT WE RUN TO THE RAVINE, AND WE REMOVE THE STONES WHICH WE HAVE PILED UPON THE IRON GRILL TO HIDE IT FROM MEN. EACH NIGHT FOR THREE HOURS, WE ARE UNDER THE EARTH, ALONE.
FROM THE HOME OF THE STREET SWEEPERS, WE HAVE STOLEN CANDLES, FLINTS, KNIVES AND PAPER, AND WE HAVE BROUGHT THEM TO THIS PLACE.
WE HAVE STOLEN GLASS VIALS, POWDERS, AND ACIDS FROM THE HOME OF THE SCHOLARS.
NOW WE SIT IN THE TUNNEL FOR THREE HOURS EACH NIGHT AND WE STUDY.
WE MELT STRANGE METALS, AND WE MIX ACIDS...
WE HAVE BUILT AN OVEN OF THE BRICKS WE GATHERED IN THE STREETS. WE BURN THE WOOD WE FIND IN THE RAVINE.
WE HAVE STOLEN MANUSCRIPTS. THIS IS A GREAT OFFENSE!

MANUSCRIPTS ARE PRECIOUS, FOR OUR BROTHERS IN THE HOME OF THE CLERKS SPEND ONE YEAR TO COPY A SINGLE SCRIPT IN THEIR CLEAR HANDWRITING.
MANUSCRIPTS ARE RARE AND THEY ARE KEPT IN THE HOME OF THE SCHOLARS.

SO WE SIT UNDER THE EARTH AND WE READ THE STOLEN SCRIPTS. TWO YEARS HAVE PASSED SINCE WE FOUND THIS PLACE. IN THESE TWO YEARS WE HAVE LEARNED MORE THAN WE HAD LEARNED IN THE TEN YEARS OF THE HOME OF THE STUDENTS.

WE HAVE LEARNED THINGS WHICH ARE NOT IN THE SCRIPTS. WE HAVE SOLVED SECRETS OF WHICH THE SCHOLARS HAVE NO KNOWLEDGE. WE HAVE COME TO SEE HOW GREAT IS THE UNEXPLORED AND MANY LIFETIMES WILL NOT BRING US TO THE END OF OUR QUEST. BUT WE WISH NO END TO OUR QUEST. WE WISH NOTHING, SAVE TO BE ALONE AND TO LEARN, AND TO FEEL AS IF WITH EACH DAY OUR SIGHT WERE GROWING SHARPER THAN THE HAWK'S AND CLEARER THAN ROCK CRYSTAL...

THE EVIL OF OUR CRIME IS NOT FOR THE HUMAN MIND TO PROBE. THE NATURE OF OUR PUNISHMENT, IF IT BE DISCOVERED, IS NOT FOR THE HUMAN HEART TO PONDER. NEVER!...NOT IN THE MEMORY OF THE ANCIENT ONES. NEVER HAVE MEN DONE THAT WHICH WE ARE DOING!

NO. THERE IS NO SHAME IN US AND NO REGRET. WE SAY TO OURSELVES THAT WE ARE A WRETCH AND A TRAITOR. BUT WE FEEL NO BURDEN UPON OUR SPIRIT, AND NO FEAR IN OUR HEART!

AND IT SEEMS TO US THAT OUR SPIRIT IS CLEAR AS A LAKE TROUBLED BY NO EYES SAVE THOSE OF THE SUN. -AND IN OUR HEART-STRANGE ARE THE WAYS OF EVIL!

--AND IN OUR HEART, THERE IS THE FIRST PEACE WE HAVE KNOWN IN TWENTY YEARS.

LIBERTY 5-3000...
LIBERTY FIVE-THREE THOUSAND...
LIBERTY 5-3000...
WE WISH TO WRITE THIS NAME. WE WISH TO SPEAK IT... BUT WE DARE NOT SPEAK IT ABOVE A WHISPER...
FOR MEN ARE FORBIDDEN TO TAKE NOTICE OF WOMEN AND WOMEN ARE FORBIDDEN TO TAKE NOTICE OF MEN.
BUT WE THINK OF ONE AMONG WOMEN. THEY WHOSE NAME IS LIBERTY 5-3000, AND WE THINK OF NO OTHERS.
THE WOMEN WHO HAVE BEEN ASSIGNED TO WORK THE SOIL LIVE IN THE HOMES OF THE PEASANTS BEYOND THE CITY.
WHERE THE CITY ENDS THERE IS A GREAT ROAD WINDING OFF TO THE NORTH, AND WE STREET SWEEPERS MUST KEEP THIS ROAD CLEAN TO THE FIRST MILEPOST.
WOMEN WORK IN THE FIELDS, AND THEIR WHITE TUNICS IN THE WIND ARE LIKE THE WINGS OF SEA-GULLS BEATING OVER THE BLACK SOIL.
AND THERE IT WAS THAT WE SAW LIBERTY 5-3000 WALKING ALONG THE FURROWS...
THEIR BODY WAS STRAIGHT AND THIN AS A BLADE OF IRON.
THEIR EYES WERE DARK AND HARD AND GLOWING, WITH NO FEAR IN THEM. NO KINDNESS AND NO GUILT.
THEIR HAIR WAS GOLDEN AS THE SUN; THEIR HAIR FLEW IN THE WIND, SHINING AND WILD, AS IF IT DEFIED MEN TO RESTRAIN IT. THEY THREW SEEDS FROM THEIR HAND AS IF THEY DEIGNED TO FLING A SCORNFUL GIFT, AND THE EARTH WAS A BEGGAR UNDER THEIR FEET...
WE STOOD STILL... FOR THE FIRST TIME DID WE KNOW FEAR, AND THEN PAIN... AND WE STOOD STILL THAT WE MIGHT NOT SPILL THIS PAIN MORE PRECIOUS THAN PLEASURE.
THEN WE HEARD A VOICE FROM THE OTHERS CALL THEIR NAME...
LIBERTY 5-3000
THUS WE LEARNED THEIR NAME.
AND WE STOOD WATCHING THEM GO, TILL THEIR WHITE TUNIC WAS IN THE BLUE MIST...

AND THE FOLLOWING DAY, AS WE CAME TO THE NORTHERN ROAD WE KEPT OUR EYES UPON LIBERTY 5-3000 IN THE FIELD.
AND EACH DAY THEREAFTER WE KNEW THE ILLNESS OF WAITING FOR OUR HOUR ON THE NORTHERN ROAD.
WE KNOW NOT WHETHER THEY LOOKED AT US ALSO BUT WE THINK THEY DID!
THEN ONE DAY THEY CAME CLOSE TO THE HEDGE, AND SUDDENLY THEY TURNED TO US.
THEY TURNED IN A WHIRL AND THE MOVEMENT OF THEIR BODY STOPPED, AS IF SLASHED OFF, AS SUDDENLY AS IT HAD STARTED. THEY STOOD STILL AS A STONE AND THEY LOOKED STRAIGHT UPON US, STRAIGHT INTO OUR EYES.
THERE WAS NO SMILE ON THEIR FACE, AND NO WELCOME. BUT THEIR FACE WAS TAUT, AND THEIR EYES WERE DARK.
THEN THEY TURNED AS SWIFTLY AND THEY WALKED AWAY FROM US.
BUT THE FOLLOWING DAY WHEN WE CAME TO THE ROAD, THEY SMILED.
THEY SMILED TO US AND FOR US. AND WE SMILED IN ANSWER.
THEIR HEAD FELL BACK, AND THEIR ARMS FELL, AS IF THEIR ARMS AND THEIR THIN WHITE NECK WERE STRICKEN SUDDENLY WITH A GREAT LASSITUDE. THEY WERE NOT LOOKING UPON US, BUT UPON THE SKY.
THEN THEY GLANCED AT US OVER THEIR SHOULDER, AND WE FELT AS IF A HAND HAD TOUCHED OUR BODY...
SLIPPING SOFTLY FROM OUR LIPS, TO OUR FEET.
EVERY MORNING THEREAFTER, WE GREETED EACH OTHER WITH OUR EYES. WE DARED NOT SPEAK. IT IS A TRANSGRESSION TO SPEAK TO MEN OF OTHER TRADES, SAVE IN GROUPS AT SOCIAL MEETINGS. BUT ONCE, STANDING AT THE HEDGE, WE RAISED OUR HAND TO OUR FOREHEAD AND THEN MOVED IT SLOWLY, PALM DOWN, TOWARD LIBERTY 5-3000.
HAD THE OTHERS SEEN IT, THEY COULD HAVE GUESSED NOTHING... FOR IT LOOKED ONLY AS IF WE WERE SHADING OUR EYES FROM THE SUN... BUT LIBERTY 5-3000 SAW IT AND UNDERSTOOD. THEY RAISED THEIR HAND TO THEIR FOREHEAD, AND MOVED IT AS WE HAD. THUS, EACH DAY WE GREET LIBERTY 5-3000 AND THEY ANSWER... AND NO MEN CAN SUSPECT.

WE DO **NOT** WONDER AT THIS *NEW* SIN OF OURS. IT IS OUR SECOND **TRANSGRESSION OF PREFERENCE**, FOR WE DO **NOT** THINK OF *ALL* OUR BROTHERS AS WE **MUST**, BUT ONLY OF **ONE**...AND THEIR NAME IS **LIBERTY 5-3000**. WE DO **NOT** KNOW **WHY** WE THINK OF THEM. WE DO **NOT** KNOW WHY, **WHEN** WE THINK OF THEM, WE FEEL OF A **SUDDEN** THAT THE **EARTH IS GOOD** AND THAT IT IS **NOT** A *BURDEN* TO **LIVE**!

AND WE TAKE **NO HEED** OF THE ***LAW*** WHICH SAYS THAT MEN MAY **NOT** THINK OF WOMEN... SAVE AT THE **TIME OF MATING**. THIS IS THE TIME EACH **SPRING** WHEN ALL THE **MEN** OLDER THAN **TWENTY** AND **ALL** THE WOMEN OLDER THAN **EIGHTEEN** ARE SENT FOR **ONE NIGHT** TO THE **CITY PALACE OF MATING**....

THE OTHER WOMEN WERE FAR OFF IN THE FIELD WHEN WE STOPPED AT THE HEDGE BY THE SIDE OF THE ROAD. THE GOLDEN ONE WERE KNEELING ALONE AT THE MOAT WHICH RUNS THROUGH THE FIELD...
THEN THE GOLDEN ONE SAW US... AND THEY DID NOT MOVE, KNEELING THERE LOOKING AT US...
CIRCLES OF LIGHT PLAYED UPON THEIR WHITE TUNIC ...FROM THE SUN ON THE WATER OF THE MOAT.
THEN THE GOLDEN ONE ROSE AND WALKED TO THE HEDGE, AS IF THEY HAD HEARD A COMMAND IN OUR EYES.
THE TWO OTHER STREET SWEEPERS OF OUR BRIGADE WERE A HUNDRED PACES AWAY DOWN THE ROAD. AND WE THOUGHT THAT INTERNATIONAL 4-8818 WOULD NOT BETRAY US, AND UNION 5-3992 WOULD NOT UNDERSTAND.
SO WE LOOKED STRAIGHT UPON THE GOLDEN ONE, AND WE SAW THE SHADOWS OF THEIR LASHES ON THEIR WHITE CHEEKS AND THE SPARKS OF THE SUN ON THEIR LIPS. AND WE SAID:
YOU ARE BEAUTIFUL LIBERTY 5-3000.
WHAT IS YOUR NAME?
EQUALITY 7-2521
YOU ARE NOT ONE OF OUR BROTHERS, EQUALITY 7-2521, FOR WE DO NOT WISH YOU TO BE.
NO, NOR ARE YOU ONE OF OUR SISTERS.
IF YOU SEE US AMONG SCORES OF WOMEN, WILL YOU LOOK UPON US?
WE SHALL LOOK UPON YOU, LIBERTY 5-3000, IF WE SEE YOU AMONG ALL THE WOMEN OF THE EARTH.
ARE STREET SWEEPERS SENT TO DIFFERENT PARTS OF THE CITY, OR DO THEY ALWAYS WORK IN THE SAME PLACES?
THEY ALWAYS WORK IN THE SAME PLACES. NO ONE WILL TAKE THIS ROAD AWAY FROM US.
YOUR EYES ARE NOT LIKE THE EYES OF ANY AMONG MEN.
AND SUDDENLY WITHOUT CAUSE FOR THE THOUGHT WHICH CAME TO US... WE FELT COLD... COLD TO OUR STOMACH.
HOW OLD ARE YOU?
THEY UNDERSTOOD OUR THOUGHT... FOR THEY LOWERED THEIR EYES FOR THE FIRST TIME.
SEVENTEEN...

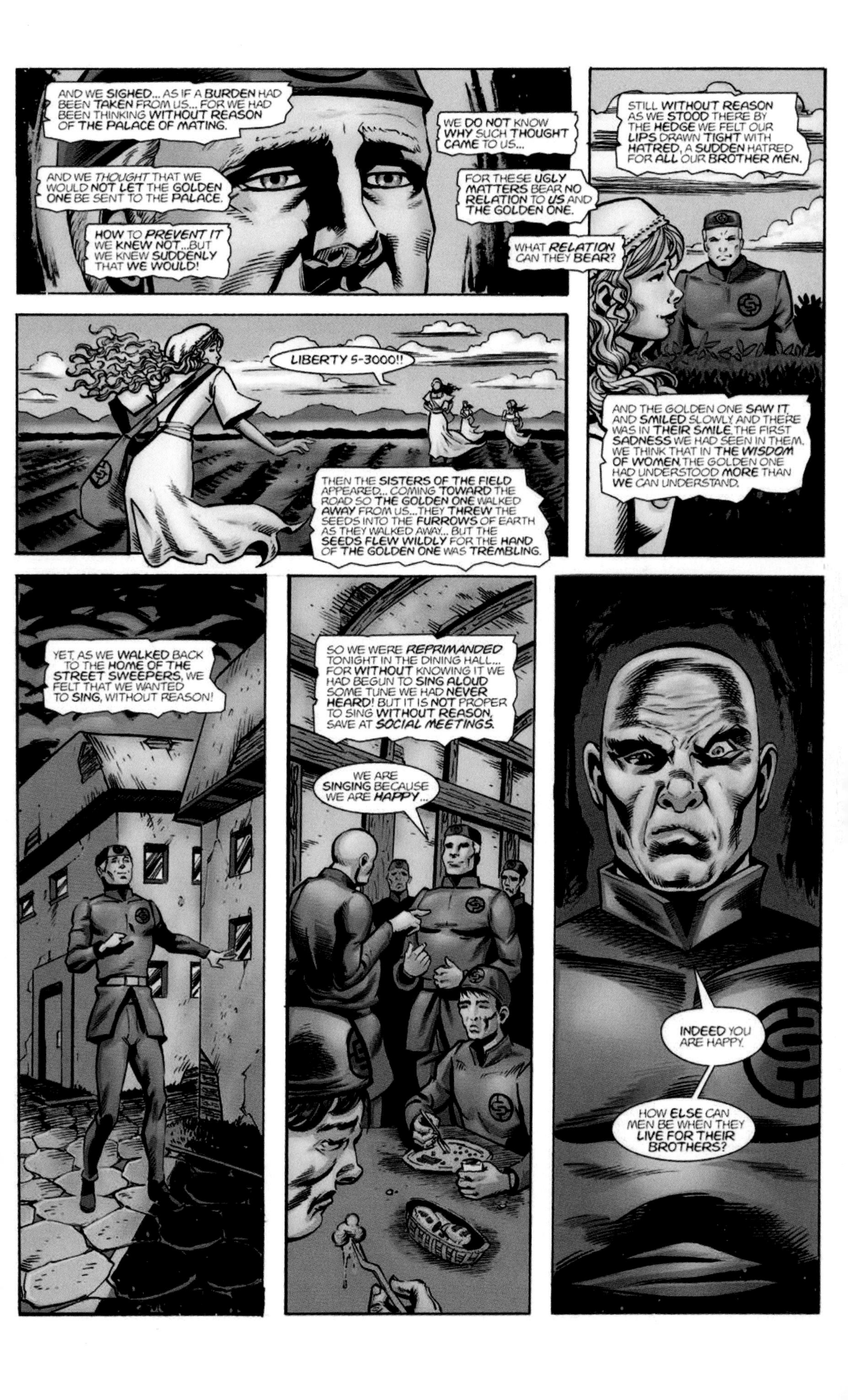
AND WE SIGHED... AS IF A BURDEN HAD BEEN TAKEN FROM US... FOR WE HAD BEEN THINKING WITHOUT REASON OF THE PALACE OF MATING.
AND WE THOUGHT THAT WE WOULD NOT LET THE GOLDEN ONE BE SENT TO THE PALACE.
HOW TO PREVENT IT WE KNEW NOT...BUT WE KNEW SUDDENLY THAT WE WOULD!
WE DO NOT KNOW WHY SUCH THOUGHT CAME TO US...
FOR THESE UGLY MATTERS BEAR NO RELATION TO US AND THE GOLDEN ONE.
STILL WITHOUT REASON AS WE STOOD THERE BY THE HEDGE WE FELT OUR LIPS DRAWN TIGHT WITH HATRED, A SUDDEN HATRED FOR ALL OUR BROTHER MEN.
WHAT RELATION CAN THEY BEAR?
AND THE GOLDEN ONE SAW IT, AND SMILED SLOWLY, AND THERE WAS IN THEIR SMILE THE FIRST SADNESS WE HAD SEEN IN THEM. WE THINK THAT IN THE WISDOM OF WOMEN, THE GOLDEN ONE HAD UNDERSTOOD MORE THAN WE CAN UNDERSTAND.
LIBERTY 5-3000!!
THEN THE SISTERS OF THE FIELD APPEARED... COMING TOWARD THE ROAD SO THE GOLDEN ONE WALKED AWAY FROM US...THEY THREW THE SEEDS INTO THE FURROWS OF EARTH AS THEY WALKED AWAY... BUT THE SEEDS FLEW WILDLY FOR THE HAND OF THE GOLDEN ONE WAS TREMBLING.
YET, AS WE WALKED BACK TO THE HOME OF THE STREET SWEEPERS, WE FELT THAT WE WANTED TO SING, WITHOUT REASON!
SO WE WERE REPRIMANDED TONIGHT IN THE DINING HALL... FOR WITHOUT KNOWING IT WE HAD BEGUN TO SING ALOUD SOME TUNE WE HAD NEVER HEARD! BUT IT IS NOT PROPER TO SING WITHOUT REASON, SAVE AT SOCIAL MEETINGS.
WE ARE SINGING BECAUSE WE ARE HAPPY...
INDEED YOU ARE HAPPY.
HOW ELSE CAN MEN BE WHEN THEY LIVE FOR THEIR BROTHERS?

AND NOW, SITTING IN OUR TUNNEL, WE WONDER ABOUT THESE WORDS. IT IS FORBIDDEN NOT TO BE HAPPY. MEN ARE FREE AND THE EARTH BELONGS TO ALL MEN; AND THE WILL OF ALL MEN TOGETHER IS GOOD FOR ALL: AND SO ALL MEN MUST BE HAPPY.
YET AS WE STAND IN THE GREAT HALL PREPARING FOR SLEEP, WE LOOK UPON OUR BROTHERS AND WE WONDER...
THE HEADS OF OUR BROTHERS ARE BOWED, THEIR EYES ARE DULL...AND NEVER DO THEY LOOK ONE ANOTHER IN THE EYES...
A WORD STEALS INTO OUR MIND AS WE LOOK UPON OUR BROTHERS, AND THAT WORD IS FEAR.
THERE IS FEAR HANGING IN THE SLEEPING HALLS AND IN THE AIR OF THE STREETS...
FEAR WALKS THROUGH THE CITY, FEAR WITHOUT NAME...WITHOUT SHAPE. ALL MEN FEEL IT AND NONE DARE TO SPEAK...
WE FEEL IT ALSO, WHEN WE ARE IN THE HOME OF THE STREET SWEEPERS...
BUT HERE IN OUR TUNNEL WE FEEL FEAR NO LONGER...
THE AIR IS PURE UNDER THE GROUND...
THERE IS NO ODOR OF MEN... AND THESE THREE HOURS GIVE US STRENGTH FOR OUR HOURS ABOVE THE GROUND.
OUR BODY IS BETRAYING US... FOR THE THE COUNCIL OF THE HOME LOOKS WITH SUSPICION UPON US.
IT IS NOT GOOD TO FEEL MUCH JOY, NOR TO BE GLAD THAT OUR BODY LIVES...
IT MUST NOT MATTER TO US WHETHER WE LIVE OR DIE, WHICH IS TO BE AS OUR BROTHERS WILL IT...
BUT WE, EQUALITY 7-2521, ARE GLAD TO BE LIVING. IF THIS IS A VICE...THEN WE WISH NO VIRTUE!!

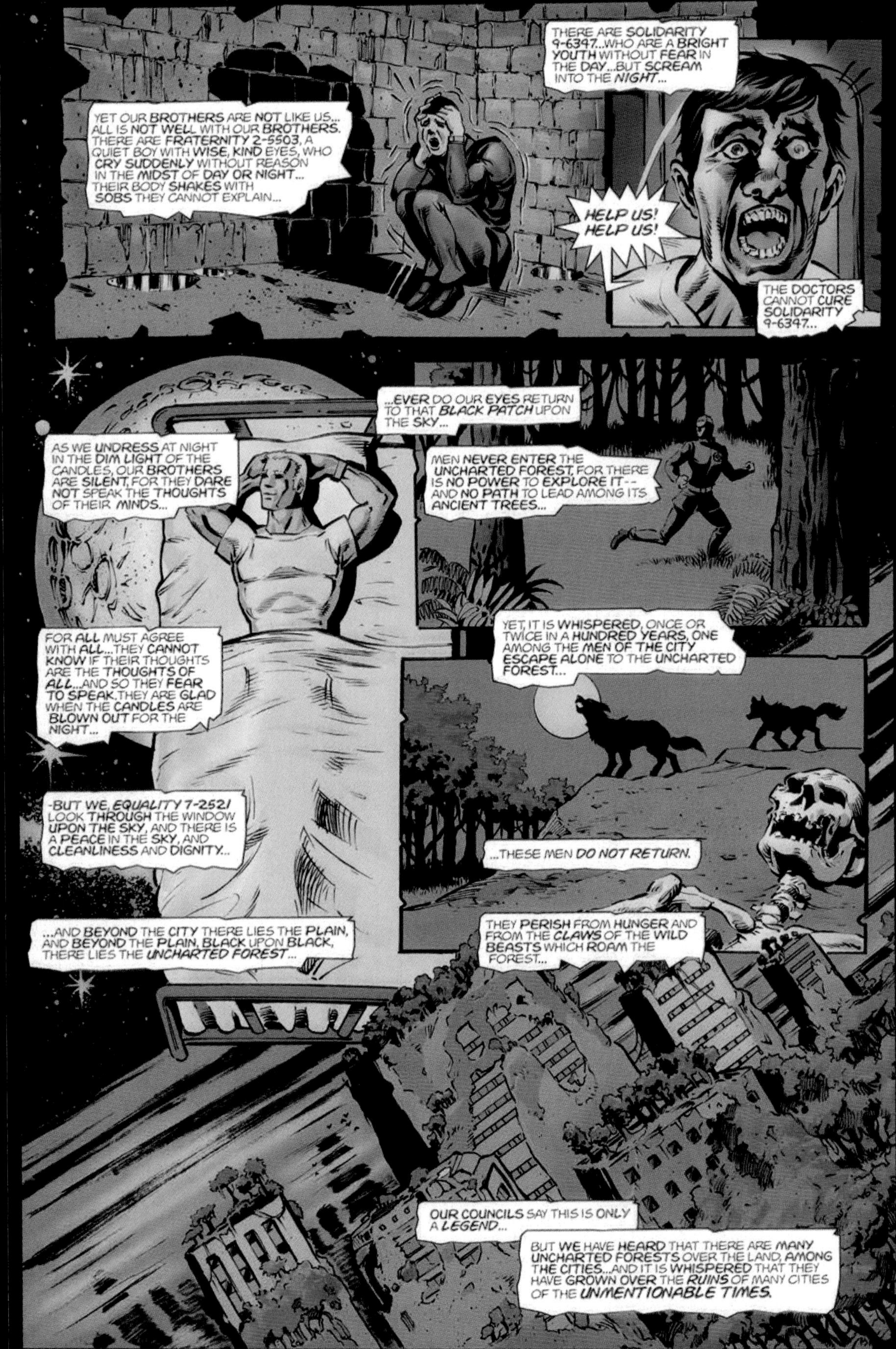
YET OUR BROTHERS ARE NOT LIKE US... ALL IS NOT WELL WITH OUR BROTHERS. THERE ARE FRATERNITY 2-5503, A QUIET BOY WITH WISE, KIND EYES, WHO CRY SUDDENLY WITHOUT REASON IN THE MIDST OF DAY OR NIGHT... THEIR BODY SHAKES WITH SOBS THEY CANNOT EXPLAIN...
THERE ARE SOLIDARITY 9-6347... WHO ARE A BRIGHT YOUTH WITHOUT FEAR IN THE DAY... BUT SCREAM INTO THE NIGHT...
HELP US! HELP US!
THE DOCTORS CANNOT CURE SOLIDARITY 9-6347...
AS WE UNDRESS AT NIGHT IN THE DIM LIGHT OF THE CANDLES, OUR BROTHERS ARE SILENT, FOR THEY DARE NOT SPEAK THE THOUGHTS OF THEIR MINDS...
FOR ALL MUST AGREE WITH ALL... THEY CANNOT KNOW IF THEIR THOUGHTS ARE THE THOUGHTS OF ALL... AND SO THEY FEAR TO SPEAK. THEY ARE GLAD WHEN THE CANDLES ARE BLOWN OUT FOR THE NIGHT...
-BUT WE, EQUALITY 7-2521 LOOK THROUGH THE WINDOW UPON THE SKY, AND THERE IS A PEACE IN THE SKY, AND CLEANLINESS AND DIGNITY...
...AND BEYOND THE CITY THERE LIES THE PLAIN, AND BEYOND THE PLAIN, BLACK UPON BLACK, THERE LIES THE UNCHARTED FOREST...
...EVER DO OUR EYES RETURN TO THAT BLACK PATCH UPON THE SKY...
MEN NEVER ENTER THE UNCHARTED FOREST, FOR THERE IS NO POWER TO EXPLORE IT-- AND NO PATH TO LEAD AMONG ITS ANCIENT TREES...
YET, IT IS WHISPERED, ONCE OR TWICE IN A HUNDRED YEARS, ONE AMONG THE MEN OF THE CITY ESCAPE ALONE TO THE UNCHARTED FOREST...
...THESE MEN DO NOT RETURN.
THEY PERISH FROM HUNGER AND FROM THE CLAWS OF THE WILD BEASTS WHICH ROAM THE FOREST...
OUR COUNCILS SAY THIS IS ONLY A LEGEND...
BUT WE HAVE HEARD THAT THERE ARE MANY UNCHARTED FORESTS OVER THE LAND, AMONG THE CITIES... AND IT IS WHISPERED THAT THEY HAVE GROWN OVER THE RUINS OF MANY CITIES OF THE UNMENTIONABLE TIMES.

FOREST WE WONDER HOW IT CAME TO PASS THAT THE SECRETS OF THE UNMENTIONABLE TIMES WERE LOST TO THE WORLD...
WE HAVE HEARD THE LEGENDS OF THE GREAT FIGHTING...IN WHICH MANY MEN FOUGHT ON ONE SIDE AND ONLY A FEW ON THE OTHER...THESE FEW WERE THE EVIL ONES...AND THEY WERE CONQUERED.
THEN GREAT FIRES RAGED OVER THE LAND... IN THESE FIRES THE EVIL ONES AND ALL THINGS MADE BY THE EVIL ONES WERE BURNED..
THE FIRE WHICH IS CALLED THE DAWN OF THE GREAT RE-BIRTH, WAS THE SCRIPT FIRE...WHERE ALL THE SCRIPTS OF THE EVIL ONES WERE BURNED...AND WITH THEM THE WORDS OF THE EVIL ONES.
ATLAS SHRUGGED AYN RAND
GREAT MOUNTAINS OF FLAME STOOD IN THE SQUARES OF THE CITIES...THEN CAME THE GREAT RE-BIRTH.
THE WORDS OF THE EVIL ONES... THE WORDS OF THE UNMENTIONABLE TIMES...
What are the words which we have lost?
MAY THE COUNCIL HAVE MERCY UPON US!! WE KNEW NOT WHAT WE WERE DOING TILL WE HAD WRITTEN IT...WE SHALL NOT ASK THIS QUESTION AND WE SHALL NOT THINK IT. WE SHALL NOT CALL DEATH UPON OUR HEAD.

AND YET...AND YET...

THERE IS ONE SINGLE WORD WHICH IS NOT IN THE LANGUAGE OF MEN... THE UNSPEAKABLE WORD WHICH NO MEN MAY SPEAK OR HEAR.

BUT SOMETIMES, SOMEWHERE, ONE AMONG MEN MAY FIND THAT WORD...UPON SCRAPS OF OLD MANUSCRIPTS OR CUT INTO FRAGMENTS OF ANCIENT STONES...

WHEN THEY SPEAK IT THEY ARE PUT TO DEATH. THERE IS NO CRIME PUNISHABLE BY DEATH IN THIS WORLD SAVE THIS ONE CRIME OF SPEAKING THE UNSPEAKABLE WORD!

WE HAVE SEEN ONE OF SUCH MEN BURNED ALIVE IN THE SQUARE OF THE CITY...AND IT WAS A SIGHT THAT HAS STAYED WITH US, AND IT HAUNTS US, AND FOLLOWS US...AND IT GIVES US NO REST...

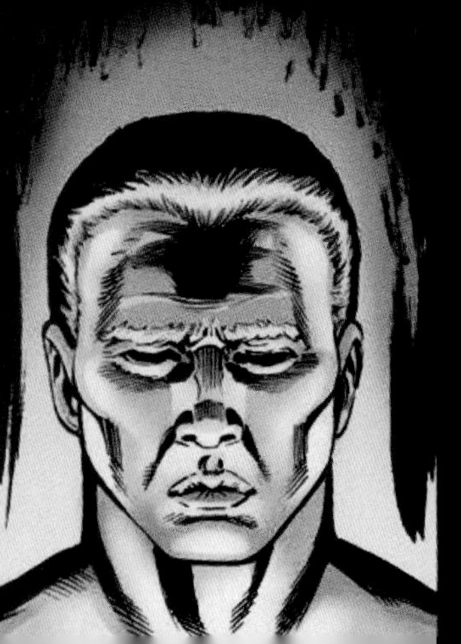

WE WERE A CHILD THEN... TEN YEARS OLD... AND WE STOOD IN THE GREAT SQUARE WITH ALL THE CHILDREN AND ALL THE MEN OF THE CITY... SENT TO BEHOLD THE BURNING.

THEY BROUGHT THE TRANSGRESSOR OUT INTO THE SQUARE AND THEY LED THEM TO THE PYRE... THEY HAD TORN OUT THE TONGUE OF THE TRANSGRESSOR... SO THAT THEY COULD SPEAK NO LONGER...
THEY WALKED TO THE PYRE, AND THEIR STEP DID NOT FALTER. OF ALL THE FACES ON THAT SQUARE... OF ALL THE FACES WHICH SHRIEKED AND SCREAMED AND SPAT CURSES UPON THEM... THEIRS WAS THE CALMEST AND THE HAPPIEST FACE.
AS THE CHAINS WERE WOUND OVER THEIR BODY AT THE STAKE... AND THE FLAME SET TO THE PYRE, THE TRANSGRESSOR LOOKED UPON THE CITY...
A MONSTROUS THOUGHT CAME TO US THEN... WHICH HAS NEVER LEFT US. WE HAD HEARD OF SAINTS... SAINTS OF LABORS AND SAINTS OF THE COUNCILS AND OF THE GREAT RE-BIRTH... BUT WE HAD NEVER SEEN A SAINT OR WHAT THE LIKENESS OF A SAINT SHOULD BE...
AND WE THOUGHT THEN THAT THE LIKENESS OF A SAINT WAS THE FACE WE SAW BEFORE US IN THE FLAMES...
...THE FACE OF THE TRANSGRESSOR OF THE UNSPEAKABLE WORD.
AS THE FLAMES ROSE A THING HAPPENED WHICH NO EYES SAW BUT OURS... THE EYES OF THE TRANSGRESSOR HAD CHOSEN US FROM THE CROWD AND WERE LOOKING STRAIGHT UPON US...
THERE WAS NO PAIN IN THEIR EYES... ONLY JOY AND PRIDE, A PRIDE HOLIER THAN IT IS FIT FOR HUMAN PRIDE TO BE!
...IT SEEMED AS IF THESE EYES WERE TRYING TO TELL US SOMETHING THROUGH THE FLAMES... AS IF THEY WERE TRYING TO SEND INTO OUR EYES SOME WORD WITHOUT SOUND...
THESE EYES WERE BEGGING US TO GATHER THAT WORD AND NOT TO LET IT GO FROM US AND FROM EARTH... BUT THE FLAMES ROSE AND WE COULD NOT GUESS THE WORD!
WHAT---EVEN IF WE HAVE TO BURN FOR IT LIKE THE SAINT OF THE PYRE---
WHAT IS THE UNSPEAKABLE WORD?
What is the Unspeakable Word?

WE, EQUALITY 7-2521... HAVE DISCOVERED A NEW POWER OF NATURE... A NEW SECRET!
THE COUNCIL OF SCHOLARS HAS SAID THAT WE ALL KNOW THE THINGS WHICH EXIST... AND THEREFORE THE THINGS WHICH ARE NOT KNOWN BY ALL DO NOT EXIST.... BUT WE THINK THE COUNCIL OF SCHOLARS IS BLIND.
THE SECRETS OF THIS EARTH ARE NOT FOR ALL MEN TO SEE...BUT ONLY FOR THOSE THAT WILL SEEK THEM...
WE HAVE WATCHED IT AND WORKED WITH IT...
...WE SAW IT FIRST TWO YEARS AGO...
ONE NIGHT WE WERE CUTTING OPEN THE BODY OF A FROG WHEN WE SAW ITS LEG JERKING...
IT WAS DEAD... YET IT MOVED!! SOME UNKNOWN POWER WAS MAKING IT MOVE!
WE COULD NOT UNDERSTAND IT... THEN AFTER MANY TESTS WE FOUND THE ANSWER...
...THE FROG HAD BEEN HANGING ON A WIRE OF COPPER; AND IT HAD BEEN THE METAL OF OUR KNIFE WHICH HAD SENT A STRANGE POWER TO THE COPPER THROUGH THE BRINE OF THE FROGS BODY!
WE PUT A PIECE OF COPPER AND A PIECE OF ZINC INTO A JAR OF BRINE...WE TOUCHED A WIRE TO THEM...
...THERE UNDER OUR FINGERS WAS A MIRACLE!...A NEW MIRACLE AND A NEW POWER!
THIS DISCOVERY HAUNTED US...WE WORKED WITH IT...WE TESTED IT... IN MORE WAYS THAN WE CAN DESCRIBE...EACH STEP WAS ANOTHER MIRACLE UNVEILING BEFORE US...
WE CAME TO KNOW THAT WE HAD FOUND THE GREATEST POWER ON EARTH!
FOR IT DEFIES ALL THE LAWS KNOWN TO MEN!
WE HAD BEEN TAUGHT WHEN STILL A CHILD... THAT THE LOADSTONE POINTS NORTH...AND THIS IS A LAW WHICH NOTHING CAN CHANGE...
YET...OUR NEW POWER DEFIES ALL LAWS.
WE FOUND THAT IT CAUSES LIGHTNING!
NEVER HAVE MEN KNOWN WHAT CAUSES LIGHTNING!
IN THUNDERSTORMS WE RAISED A TALL ROD OF IRON BY THE SIDE OF OUR HOLE...
WE HAVE SEEN THE LIGHTNING STRIKE AGAIN AND AGAIN...
NOW WE KNOW THAT METAL DRAWS THE POWER OF THE SKY... AND THAT METAL CAN BE MADE TO GIVE IT FORTH!

WE HAVE BUILT STRANGE THINGS WITH THIS DISCOVERY OF OURS. WE USED FOR IT THE COPPER WIRES WHICH WE FOUND HERE UNDER THE GROUND.

WE HAVE WALKED THE LENGTH OF OUR TUNNEL WITH A CANDLE LIGHTING THE WAY... WE COULD GO NO FARTHER THAN HALF A MILE, FOR EARTH AND ROCK HAD FALLEN AT BOTH ENDS.

BUT WE GATHERED ALL THE THINGS WE FOUND AND WE BROUGHT THEM TO OUR WORK PLACE... WE FOUND STRANGE BOXES WITH BARS OF METAL INSIDE, WITH MANY CORDS AND STRANDS AND COILS OF METAL.

WE FOUND WIRES THAT LED TO STRANGE LITTLE GLOBES OF GLASS ON THE WALLS... THEY CONTAINED THREADS OF METAL THINNER THAN A SPIDER'S WEB.

THESE THINGS HELP US IN OUR WORK. WE DO NOT UNDERSTAND THEM, BUT WE THINK THAT THE MEN OF THE UNMENTIONABLE TIMES HAD KNOWN OUR POWER OF THE SKY, AND THESE THINGS HAD SOME RELATION TO IT. WE DO NOT KNOW... BUT WE SHALL LEARN! WE CANNOT STOP NOW, EVEN THOUGH IT FRIGHTENS US THAT WE ARE ALONE IN OUR KNOWLEDGE.

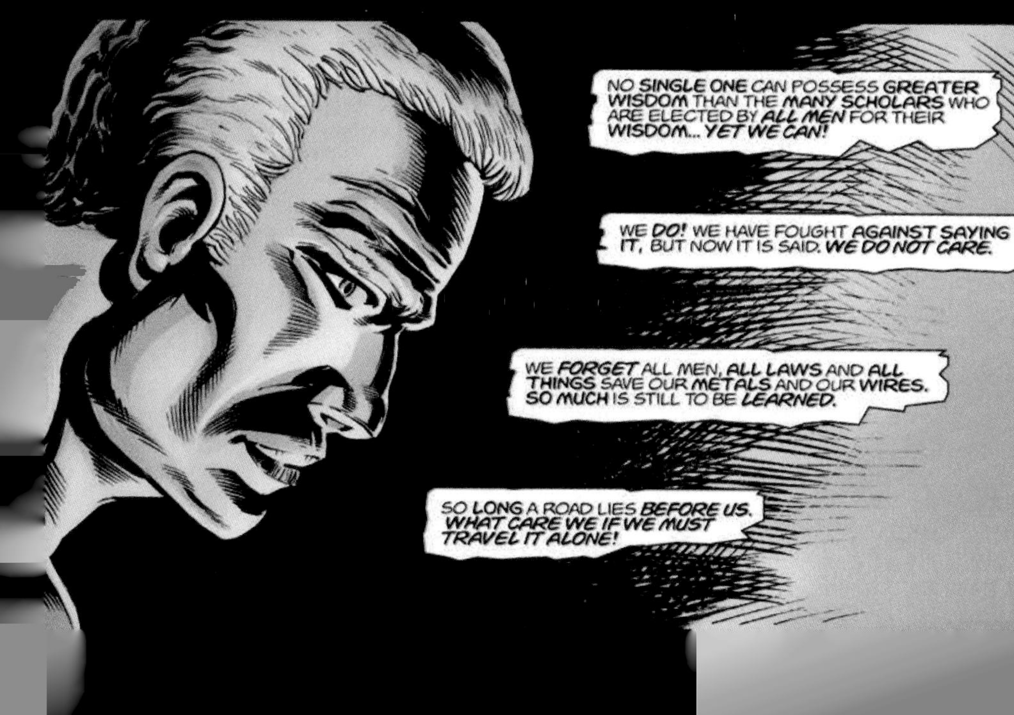

NO SINGLE ONE CAN POSSESS GREATER WISDOM THAN THE MANY SCHOLARS WHO ARE ELECTED BY ALL MEN FOR THEIR WISDOM... YET WE CAN!
WE DO! WE HAVE FOUGHT AGAINST SAYING IT, BUT NOW IT IS SAID. WE DO NOT CARE.
WE FORGET ALL MEN, ALL LAWS AND ALL THINGS SAVE OUR METALS AND OUR WIRES. SO MUCH IS STILL TO BE LEARNED.
SO LONG A ROAD LIES BEFORE US. WHAT CARE WE IF WE MUST TRAVEL IT ALONE!

MANY DAYS PASSED BEFORE WE COULD SPEAK TO THE GOLDEN ONE AGAIN.
THE WOMEN OF THE FIELD WERE WEARY. THEY TARRIED OVER THEIR WORK AND THEY WERE FAR FROM THE ROAD WHEN WE CAME.
BUT THE GOLDEN ONE STOOD ALONE AT THE HEDGE...WAITING.
THEN CAME THE DAY WHEN THE SKY TURNED WHITE, AS IF THE SUN HAD BURST AND SPREAD ITS FLAME IN THE AIR, AND THE FIELDS LAY STILL WITHOUT BREATH...
WE STOPPED AND WE SAW THAT THEIR EYES, SO HARD AND SCORNFUL TO THE WORLD, WERE LOOKING AT US AS IF THEY WOULD OBEY ANY WORD THAT WE MIGHT SPEAK.
WE HAVE GIVEN YOU A NAME IN OUR THOUGHTS LIBERTY 5-3000.
WHAT IS OUR NAME?
THE GOLDEN ONE.
NOR DO WE CALL YOU EQUALITY 7-2521 WHEN WE THINK OF YOU.
WHAT NAME HAVE YOU GIVEN US?
THE UNCONQUERED.

SUCH THOUGHTS AS THESE ARE FORBIDDEN, GOLDEN ONE.
BUT YOU THINK SUCH THOUGHTS AS THESE AND YOU WISH US TO THINK THEM.
WE LOOKED INTO THEIR EYES AND WE COULD NOT LIE.
YES.
OUR DEAREST ONE...
DO NOT OBEY US.
SPEAK THESE WORDS AGAIN...
WHICH WORDS?
BUT THEY DID NOT ANSWER AND WE KNEW IT.
OUR DEAREST ONE...
NEVER HAVE MEN SAID THIS TO WOMEN.
THE HEAD OF THE GOLDEN ONE BOWED SLOWLY AND THEY STOOD STILL BEFORE US... AS IF THEIR BODY WERE DELIVERED IN SUBMISSION TO OUR EYES.
WE COULD NOT SPEAK.
THEN THEY RAISED THEIR HEAD AND THEY SPOKE SIMPLY AND GENTLY AS IF THEY WISHED US TO FORGET SOME ANXIETY OF THEIR OWN.
THE DAY IS HOT, AND YOU HAVE WORKED FOR MANY HOURS... YOU MUST BE WEARY.

NO...
IT IS COOLER IN THE FIELDS...
AND THERE IS WATER TO DRINK. ARE YOU THIRSTY?
WE SHALL BRING THE WATER TO YOU...
YES, BUT WE CANNOT CROSS THE HEDGE.
THEN THEY KNELT BY THE MOAT, THEY GATHERED WATER IN THEIR TWO HANDS.
WE DO NOT KNOW IF WE DRANK THAT WATER.
WE ONLY KNEW SUDDENLY THAT THEIR HANDS WERE EMPTY, BUT WE WERE STILL HOLDING OUR LIPS TO THEIR HANDS, AND THAT THEY KNEW IT, BUT DID NOT MOVE.
WE RAISED OUR HEAD AND STEPPED BACK.
FOR WE DID NOT UNDERSTAND WHAT HAD MADE US DO THIS, AND WE WERE AFRAID TO UNDERSTAND IT.
AND THE GOLDEN ONE STEPPED BACK, AND STOOD LOOKING UPON THEIR HANDS IN WONDER.
THEN THE GOLDEN ONE MOVED AWAY.
EVEN THOUGH NO OTHERS WERE COMING THEY MOVED STEPPING BACK, AS IF THEY COULD NOT TURN FROM US, THEIR ARMS BENT BEFORE THEM, AS IF THEY COULD NOT LOWER THEIR HANDS.

WE MADE IT. WE CREATED IT. WE BROUGHT IT FORTH FROM THE NIGHT OF THE AGES. WE ALONE. OUR HANDS. OUR MIND. OURS ALONE AND ONLY.
TRIALS THAN WE CAN COUNT, W FINISHED BUILDING A STRANGE THING...FROM THE REMAINS OF THE UNMENTIONABLE TIMES, BOX OF GLASS, DEVISED TO GIV FORTH THE POWER OF THE SK OF GREATER STRENGTH THAN WE HAD EVER ACHIEVED BEFOR
WE KNOW NOT WHAT WE ARE SAYING. OUR HEAD IS REELING. WE LOOK UPON THE LIGHT WHICH WE HAVE MADE. WE SHALL BE FORGIVEN FOR ANYTHING WE SAY TONIGHT...
WHEN WE PUT OUR WIRES TO THIS BOX, WHEN WE CLOSED THE CURREN THE WIRE GLOWED! IT CAME TO LIF IT TURNED RED, AND A CIRCLE OF LIGHT LAY ON THE STONE BEFORE US
WE COULD NOT CONCEIVE OF THAT WHICH WE HAD CREATED. WE HAD TOUCHED NO FLINT... MADE NO FIRE. YET HERE WAS LIGHT!... LIGHT THAT CAME FROM NOWHERE! LIGHT FROM THE HEART OF METAL!!
WE BLEW OUT THE CANDLE. DARKNES SWALLOWED US. THERE WAS NOTHING LEFT AROUND US. NOTHING SAVE NIGH AND A THIN THREAD OF FLAME IN IT AS A CRACK IN THE WALL OF A PRISON.
WE STRETCHED OUR HANDS TO WIRE AND WE SAW OUR FINGERS THE RED GLOW...IN THAT MOME NOTHING EXISTED SAVE OUR TW HANDS OVER A WIRE... GLOWING THE BLACK ABYSS.
THEN WE THOUGHT OF THE MEANING OF THAT WHICH LAY BEFORE US...
WE CAN LIGHT OUR TUNNEL AND THE CITY AND ALL THE CITIES OF THE WORLD WITH NOTHING SAVE METAL AND WIRES! WE CAN GIVE OUR BROTHERS A NEW LIGHT, CLEANER AND BRIGHTER THAN ANY THEY HAVE KNOWN... THE POWER OF THE SKY CAN BE MADE TO DO MEN'S BIDDING!

THEN WE KNEW WHAT WE MUST DO... OUR DISCOVERY IS TOO GREAT FOR US TO WASTE OUR TIME IN SWEEPING THE STREETS. WE MUST NOT KEEP OUR SECRET TO OURSELVES, NOR BURIED UNDER THE GROUND... WE MUST BRING IT INTO THE SIGHT OF ALL MEN! WE NEED THE WORK ROOMS OF THE HOME OF THE SCHOLARS. WE WANT THE HELP OF OUR BROTHER SCHOLARS AND THEIR WISDOM JOINED TO OURS.
IN A MONTH THE WORLD COUNCIL OF SCHOLARS IS TO MEET IN OUR CITY... IT IS A GREAT COUNCIL TO WHICH THE WISEST OF ALL LANDS ARE ELECTED. WE SHALL GO TO THIS COUNCIL, AND WE SHALL LAY BEFORE THEM AS OUR GIFT, THE GLASS BOX WITH THE POWER OF THE SKY!
BUT NEITHER HAS A GIFT SUCH AS OURS EVER BEEN OFFERED TO MEN!
WE SHALL CONFESS EVERYTHING. THEY WILL SEE, UNDERSTAND AND FORGIVE...FOR OUR GIFT IS GREATER THAN OUR TRANSGRESSION.
THEY WILL EXPLAIN IT TO THE COUNCIL OF VOCATIONS AND WE SHALL BE ASSIGNED TO THE HOME OF THE SCHOLARS...THIS HAS NEVER BEEN DONE BEFORE..
WE MUST WAIT... WE MUST GUARD OUR TUNNEL AS WE HAD NEVER GUARDED IT BEFORE...FOR SHOULD ANY MEN, SAVE THE SCHOLARS, LEARN OF OUR SECRET, THEY WOULD NOT UNDERSTAND IT, NOR WOULD THEY BELIEVE US. THEY WOULD SEE NOTHING SAVE OUR CRIME. THEY WOULD DESTROY US AND OUR LIGHT.
WE CARE NOT ABOUT OUR BODY, BUT OUR LIGHT IS...

YES. WE DO CARE! FOR THE FIRST TIME WE DO CARE ABOUT OUR BODY...
FOR THIS WIRE IS AS A PART OF OUR BODY AS A VEIN TORN FROM US, GLOWING WITH OUR BLOOD... ARE WE PROUD OF THIS THREAD OF METAL OR OF OUR HANDS WHICH MADE IT?... OR IS THERE A LINE TO DIVIDE THESE TWO?

FOR THE FIRST TIME WE DO KNOW HOW STRONG OUR ARMS ARE... AND A STRANGE THOUGHT COMES TO US...
FOR THE FIRST TIME IN OUR LIFE WE WONDER WHAT WE LOOK LIKE...
MEN NEVER SEE THEIR OWN FACES, FOR IT IS EVIL TO HAVE CONCERN FOR THEIR OWN FACES OR BODIES... BUT TONIGHT, FOR

WE HAVE NOT WRITTEN FOR THIRTY DAYS.... FOR THIRTY DAYS WE HAVE NOT BEEN HERE IN OUR TUNNEL. WE HAD BEEN CAUGHT!
IT HAPPENED ON THAT NIGHT WHEN WE WROTE LAST. WE FORGOT THAT NIGHT TO WATCH THE SAND IN THE GLASS WHICH TELLS US WHEN THREE HOURS HAVE PASSED AND IT IS TIME TO RETURN TO THE CITY THEATRE...
WHEN WE REMEMBERED IT... THE SAND HAD RUN OUT!
WE HASTENED TO THE THEATRE. BUT THE BIG TENT STOOD GREY. THE STREETS OF THE CITY LAY BEFORE US...DARK AND EMPTY.
IF WE WENT BACK TO HIDE IN OUR TUNNEL WE WOULD BE FOUND AND OUR LIGHT FOUND WITH US...SO WE WENT TO THE HOME OF THE STREET SWEEPERS.
WHEN THE COUNCIL OF THE HOME QUESTIONED US... WE LOOKED UPON THE FACES OF THE COUNCIL, BUT THERE WAS NO CURIOUSITY IN THOSE FACES, NO MERCY...
WHERE HAVE YOU BEEN?!
WE THOUGHT OF OUR GLASS BOX AND OF OUR LIGHT, AND WE FORGOT ALL ELSE...
WE WILL NOT TELL YOU.
THE OLDEST DID NOT QUESTION US FURTHER...THEY TURNED TO THE TWO YOUNGEST...
TAKE OUR BROTHER EQUALITY 7-2521 TO THE PALACE OF CORRECTIVE DETENTION.
LASH THEM UNTIL THEY TELL.

SO WE WERE TAKEN TO THE STONE ROOM UNDER THE PALACE OF CORRECTIVE DETENTION...
TWO JUDGES STOOD IN A CORNER OF THE ROOM... THEY GAVE THE SIGNAL TO THE TWO STRONG HOODED ONES...
THEY TORE OUR CLOTHES FROM OUR BODY...THEY THREW US DOWN UPON OUR KNEES AND THEY CHAINED OUR HANDS TO THE POST...
THE FIRST BLOW OF THE LASH FELT AS IF OUR SPINE HAD BEEN CUT IN TWO.
THE SECOND BLOW STOPPED THE FIRST. ... FOR A SECOND WE FELT NOTHING.. THEN THE PAIN STRUCK US IN OUR THROAT.
FIRE RAN IN OUR LUNGS WITHOUT AIR...
BUT WE DID NOT CRY OUT.
THE LASH WHISTLED LIKE A SINGING WIND...
WE TRIED TO COUNT THE BLOWS BUT WE LOST COUNT...WE KNEW THAT THE BLOWS WERE FALLING UPON OUR BACK... ONLY WE FELT NOTHING UPON OUR BACK ANY LONGER...
A FLAMING GRILL KEPT DANCING BEFORE OUR EYES...
WE THOUGHT OF NOTHING SAVE THAT GRILL... A GRILL, A GRILL, A GRILL OF RED SQUARES... AND THEN WE KNEW THAT WE WERE LOOKING AT THE SQUARES OF THE IRON GRILL IN THE DOOR...
THERE WERE ALSO THE SQUARES OF BRICK ON WALLS...AND THE SQUARES WHICH THE LASH WAS CUTTING UPON OUR BACK...CROSSING AND RE-CROSSING ITSELF IN OUR FLESH.

WE SAW THE RED FROTH OF OUR MOUTH ON THE WITHERED FINGERS... AND THE JUDGE ASKED:
...THEN WE SAW A FIST BEFORE US.
WHERE HAVE YOU BEEN?
BUT WE JERKED OUR HEAD AWAY...AND HID OUR FACE UPON OUR CHAINED HANDS... AND BIT OUR LIPS...
THE LASH WHISTLED AGAIN...
WE KNEW NOTHING, SAVE TWO VOICES SNARLING STEADILY...
WE WONDERED WHO WAS SPRINKLING BURNING COAL DUST UPON THE FLOOR...FOR WE SAW DROPS OF RED TWINKLING ON THE GROUND AROUND US..
ONE AFTER THE OTHER... EVEN THOUGH WE KNEW THEY WERE SPEAKING MANY MINUTES APART:
WHERE HAVE YOU BEEN???
WHERE? WHERE? WHERE?
OUR LIPS MOVED... BUT THE SOUND TRICKLED BACK INTO OUR THROAT AND THE SOUND WAS ONLY:
THE LIGHT... THE LIGHT... THE LIGHT...
THEN WE KNEW NOTHING.

WE OPENED OUR EYES LYING ON THE FLOOR OF A CELL.
WE LOOKED UPON TWO HANDS LYING FAR BEFORE US ON THE BRICKS...WE MOVED THEM AND WE KNEW THAT THEY WERE OUR HANDS...
WE LAY IN OUR CELL FOR MANY DAYS...
WE COULD NOT MOVE OUR BODY. THEN WE SMILED... FOR WE THOUGHT OF OUR LIGHT... AND THAT WE HAD NOT BETRAYED IT.
THE DOOR OPENED TWICE EACH DAY...
ONCE FOR THE MEN WHO BROUGHT US BREAD AND WATER...AND ONCE FOR THE JUDGES.
MANY JUDGES CAME TO OUR CELL... FIRST THE HUMBLEST AND THEN THE MOST HONORED JUDGES OF THE CITY...
THEY STOOD BEFORE US IN THEIR WHITE TOGAS AND THEY ASKED:
ARE YOU READY TO SPEAK?
BUT WE SHOOK OUR HEAD... LYING BEFORE THEM ON THE FLOOR.
...AND THEY DEPARTED.
WE COUNTED EACH DAY AND EACH NIGHT AS IT PASSED. THEN, TONIGHT WE KNEW WE MUST ESCAPE...FOR TOMORROW THE WORLD COUNCIL OF SCHOLARS IS TO MEET IN OUR CITY...

IT WAS EASY TO ESCAPE FROM THE PALACE OF CORRECTIVE DETENTION... THE LOCKS ARE OLD ON THE DOORS AND THERE ARE NO GUARDS ABOUT. THERE IS NO REASON TO HAVE GUARDS, FOR MEN HAVE NEVER DEFIED THE COUNCILS SO FAR AS TO ESCAPE FROM WHATEVER PLACE THEY WERE ORDERED TO BE.
OUR BODY IS HEALTHY, AND STRENGTH RETURNS TO IT SPEEDILY.
WE LUNGED AGAINST THE DOOR... AND IT GAVE WAY.
WE STOLE THROUGH THE DARK PASSAGES AND THROUGH THE DARK STREETS AND DOWN INTO OUR TUNNEL.
WE LIT THE CANDLE AND WE SAW THAT OUR PLACE HAD NOT BEEN FOUND AND NOTHING HAD BEEN TOUCHED.
AND OUR GLASS BOX STOOD BEFORE US ON THE COLD OVEN, AS WE HAD LEFT IT.
TOMORROW, IN THE FULL LIGHT OF DAY, WE SHALL TAKE OUR BOX AND LEAVE OUR TUNNEL OPEN... AND WALK THROUGH THE STREETS TO THE HOME OF THE SCHOLARS.
WHAT MATTER THEY NOW... THE SCARS UPON OUR BACK!
WE SHALL PUT BEFORE THEM THE GREATEST GIFT EVER OFFERED TO MEN. WE SHALL HAND TO THEM AS OUR CONFESSION THESE PAGES WE HAVE WRITTEN.
WE SHALL JOIN OUR HANDS TO THEIRS, AND WE SHALL WORK TOGETHER, WITH THE POWER OF THE SKY, FOR THE GLORY OF MANKIND.
OUR BLESSING UPON YOU, OUR BROTHERS! TOMORROW YOU WILL TAKE US BACK INTO YOUR FOLD AND WE SHALL BE AN OUTCAST NO LONGER.
TOMORROW WE SHALL BE ONE OF YOU AGAIN.
TOMORROW!!

IT IS DARK HERE IN THE FOREST.
THE LEAVES RUSTLE OVER OUR HEAD... BLACK AGAINST THE LAST GOLD OF THE SKY.
THE MOSS IS SOFT AND WARM. WE SHALL SLEEP ON THIS MOSS FOR MANY NIGHTS... TILL THE BEASTS OF THE FOREST COME TO TEAR OUR BODY.
WE HAVE NO BED NOW, SAVE THE MOSS AND NO FUTURE SAVE THE BEASTS.
WE ARE OLD NOW-- YET WE WERE YOUNG THIS MORNING WHEN WE CARRIED OUR GLASS BOX THROUGH THE STREETS OF THE CITY TO THE HOME OF THE SCHOLARS.
NO MEN STOPPED US... FOR THERE WERE NONE ABOUT FROM THE PALACE OF CORRECTIVE DETENTION AND THE OTHERS KNEW NOTHING. NO MEN STOPPED US AT THE GATE.
WE WALKED TO THE GREAT HALL WHERE THE WORLD COUNCIL OF SCHOLARS SAT IN SOLEMN MEETING.
WE SAW THE SCHOLARS WHO SAT AROUND A LONG TABLE. THERE WERE MEN WHOSE FAMOUS NAMES WE KNEW AND OTHERS FROM DISTANT LANDS WHOSE NAMES WE HAD NOT HEARD.
WE SAW A GREAT PAINTING ON THE WALL OVER THEIR HEADS OF THE TWENTY ILLUSTRIOUS MEN WHO HAD INVENTED THE CANDLE.
THESE GREAT AND WISE OF THE EARTH DID NOT KNOW WHAT TO THINK OF US... AND THEY LOOKED UPON US WITH WONDER AND CURIOSITY, AS IF WE WERE A MIRACLE.
OUR GREETING TO YOU, OUR HONORED BROTHERS OF THE WORLD COUNCIL OF SCHOLARS!

THEN COLLECTIVE 0-0009 THE OLDEST AND WISEST OF THE COUNCIL SPOKE AND ASKED--
WHO ARE YOU, OUR BROTHER? FOR YOU DO NOT LOOK LIKE A SCHOLAR.
OUR NAME IS EQUALITY 7-2521
AND WE ARE A STREET SWEEPER OF THIS CITY.
THEN IT WAS AS IF A GREAT WIND HAD STRICKEN THE HALL-- FOR ALL THE SCHOLARS SPOKE AT ONCE, AND THEY WERE ANGRY AND FRIGHTENED.
A STREET SWEEPER!
A STREET SWEEPER WALKING IN UPON THE WORLD COUNCIL OF SCHOLARS!
IT IS NOT TO BE BELIEVED!!
IT IS AGAINST ALL RULES AND ALL LAWS!
BUT WE KNEW HOW TO STOP THEM...
OUR BROTHERS!
WE MATTER NOT... NOR OUR TRANSGRESSION.
IT IS ONLY OUR BROTHER MEN WHO MATTER. GIVE NO THOUGHT TO US... FOR WE ARE NOTHING-- BUT LISTEN TO OUR WORDS. FOR WE BRING YOU A GIFT SUCH AS HAS NEVER BEEN BROUGHT TO MEN. LISTEN TO US, FOR WE HOLD THE FUTURE OF MANKIND IN OUR HANDS.
THEN THEY LISTENED.

WE PLACED OUR GLASS BOX UPON THE TABLE BEFORE THEM.
WE SPOKE OF IT AND OF OUR LONG QUEST... AND OF OUR TUNNEL AND OF OUR ESCAPE FROM THE PALACE OF CORRECTIVE DETENTION.
NOT A HAND MOVED IN THAT HALL AS WE SPOKE...NOR AN EYE.
THEN WE PUT WIRES TO THE BOX...
AND THEY ALL BENT FORWARD AND SAT STILL-- WATCHING.
AND SLOWLY... SLOWLY AS A FLUSH OF BLOOD... A RED FLAME TREMBLED IN THE WIRE.
THEN THE WIRE GLOWED.
BUT TERROR STRUCK THE MEN OF THE COUNCIL.
THEY LEAPT TO THEIR FEET... THEY RAN FROM THE TABLE AND THEY STOOD PRESSED AGAINST THE WALL-- HUDDLED TOGETHER... SEEKING THE WARMTH OF ONE ANOTHER'S BODIES TO GIVE THEM COURAGE.
WE LOOKED UPON THEM AND WE LAUGHED AND SAID:
FEAR NOTHING OUR BROTHERS.
THERE IS A GREAT POWER IN THESE WIRES-- BUT THIS POWER IS TAMED. IT IS YOURS. WE GIVE IT TO YOU.
STILL THEY DID NOT MOVE.
WE GIVE YOU THE POWER OF THE SKY!
WE GIVE YOU THE KEY TO THE EARTH!
LET US ALL WORK TOGETHER AND HARNESS THIS POWER AND MAKE IT EASE THE TOIL OF MEN.
TAKE IT, AND LET US BE ONE OF YOU... THE HUMBLEST AMONG YOU.
LET US THROW AWAY OUR CANDLES AND OUR TORCHES. LET US FLOOD OUR CITIES WITH LIGHT. LET US BRING A NEW LIGHT TO MEN!

BUT THEY LOOKED UPON US AND SUDDENLY WE WERE AFRAID.
FOR THEIR EYES WERE STILL, AND SMALL AND EVIL.
OUR BROTHERS!
HAVE YOU NOTHING TO SAY TO US?
YES, WE HAVE MUCH TO SAY TO YOU.
THE SOUND OF THEIR VOICE BROUGHT SILENCE TO THE HALL, AND TO THE BEAT OF OUR HEART.
YES, WE HAVE MUCH TO SAY TO A WRETCH WHO HAVE BROKEN ALL LAWS AND WHO BOAST OF THEIR INFAMY.
HOW DARED YOU THINK THAT YOUR MIND HELD GREATER WISDOM THAN THE MINDS OF YOUR BROTHERS! AND IF THE COUNCILS HAD DECREED THAT YOU SHOULD BE A STREET SWEEPER, HOW DARED YOU THINK THAT YOU COULD BE OF GREATER USE TO MEN THAN IN SWEEPING THE STREETS?
HOW DARED YOU, GUTTER CLEANER!! TO HOLD YOURSELF AS ONE ALONE AND WITH THE THOUGHTS OF THE ONE AND NOT THE MANY?
YOU SHALL BE BURNED AT THE STAKE!
NO! THEY SHALL BE LASHED! TILL THERE IS NOTHING LEFT UNDER THE LASHES!
OUR BROTHERS! YOU ARE RIGHT. LET THE WILL OF THE COUNCIL BE DONE UPON MY BODY. BUT THE LIGHT? WHAT WILL YOU DO WITH THE LIGHT?
SO... YOU THINK YOU HAVE FOUND A NEW POWER. DO ALL YOUR BROTHERS THINK THAT?
NO.
WHAT IS NOT THOUGHT BY ALL MEN CANNOT BE TRUE.

YOU HAVE WORKED ON THIS **ALONE?**
YES...
WHAT IS **NOT** DONE COLLECTIVELY **CANNOT** BE GOOD...

MANY MEN IN THE HOMES OF THE SCHOLARS HAVE HAD **STRANGE** NEW IDEAS IN THE PAST... BUT WHEN THE MAJORITY OF THEIR BROTHER SCHOLARS VOTED AGAINST THEM... THEY **ABANDONED** THEIR IDEAS AS **ALL** MEN MUST.
THIS BOX IS **USELESS...**
SHOULD IT BE WHAT THEY **CLAIM** OF IT...THEN IT WOULD **BRING RUIN** TO THE **DEPARTMENT OF THE CANDLES.**
THE **CANDLE** IS A GREAT **BOON** TO MANKIND... AS APPROVED BY **ALL MEN.** THEREFORE IT **CANNOT** BE DESTROYED BY THE ***WHIM OF ONE.***
THIS WOULD **WRECK THE PLANS** OF THE **WORLD COUNCIL**--AND WITHOUT PLANS OF THE WORLD COUNCIL, THE SUN **CANNOT** RISE. IT TOOK **FIFTY YEARS** TO SECURE THE **APPROVAL** OF ALL THE COUNCILS FOR THE CANDLE...AND TO DECIDE UPON THE **NUMBER** NEEDED... AND TO **RE-FIT** THE PLANS SO AS TO MAKE **CANDLES** INSTEAD OF **TORCHES. THIS TOUCHED UPON THOUSANDS** AND **THOUSANDS** OF MEN WORKING IN **SCORES OF STATES.** WE **CANNOT** ALTER THE PLANS AGAIN SO SOON.
AND IF THIS SHOULD **LIGHTEN** THE TOIL OF MEN, THEN IT IS A ***GREAT EVIL,*** FOR MEN HAVE **NO CAUSE** TO EXIST, **SAVE** IN TOILING FOR **OTHER MEN.**

THIS THING...
MUST BE...
DESTROYED!!
AND ALL THE OTHERS CRIED AS ONE:
DESTROYED!
MUST BE DESTROYED!
DEST
MUST BE DESTROYED!
WE SHOVED THEM ASIDE... AND WE RAN TO THE WINDOW.
WE TURNED AND WE LOOKED AT THEM FOR THE LAST TIME, AND A RAGE, SUCH AS IT IS NOT FIT FOR HUMANS TO KNOW, CHOKED OUR VOICE IN OUR THROAT.
YOU FOOLS!
YOU FOOLS!
YOU THRICE-DAMNED FOOLS!

WE SWUNG OUR FIST THROUGH THE WINDOW PANE...
...AND WE LEAPT OUT OF THE RINGING RAIN OF GLASS!

WE FELL...
BUT WE NEVER LET THE BOX FALL FROM OUR HANDS.
THEN WE RAN...

MEN AND HOUSES STREAKED PAST US IN A TORRENT WITHOUT SHAPE.

BUT WE RAN.
WE KNEW NOT WHERE WE WERE GOING.
WE KNEW ONLY THAT WE MUST RUN ...RUN TO THE END OF THE WORLD, TO THE END OF OUR DAYS.
THEN WE KNEW SUDDENLY THAT WE WERE LYING ON A SOFT EARTH AND THAT WE HAD STOPPED.
TREES TALLER THAN WE HAD EVER SEEN BEFORE STOOD OVER US IN A GREAT SILENCE... THEN WE KNEW. WE WERE IN THE UNCHARTED FOREST. WE HAD NOT THOUGHT OF COMING HERE... BUT OUR LEGS HAD CARRIED OUR WISDOM...AND OUR LEGS HAD BROUGHT US TO THE UNCHARTED FOREST AGAINST OUR WILL.

...BUT AS IF IT WERE LEAPING UP TO MEET US... WE WAITED FOR THE EARTH TO RISE AND STRIKE US IN THE FACE.
OUR GLASS BOX LAY BESIDE US. WE CRAWLED TO IT--WE FELL UPON IT...OUR FACE IN OUR ARMS, AND WE LAY STILL.
WE LAY THUS FOR A LONG TIME. THEN WE ROSE... WE TOOK OUR BOX AND WALKED INTO THE FOREST.
IT MATTERED NOT WHERE WE WENT. WE KNEW THAT MEN WOULD NOT FOLLOW US-- FOR THEY NEVER ENTER THE UNCHARTED FOREST. WE HAD NOTHING TO FEAR FROM THEM. THE FOREST DISPOSES OF ITS OWN VICTIMS. THIS GAVE US NO FEAR EITHER... ONLY WE WISHED TO BE AWAY--AWAY FROM THE CITY AND FROM THE AIR THAT TOUCHES UPON THE AIR OF THE CITY.
SO WE WALKED ON...OUR BOX IN OUR ARMS-- OUR HEART EMPTY.

WE ARE DOOMED. WHATEVER DAYS ARE LEFT TO US...WE SHALL SPEND THEM ALONE.
WE HAVE HEARD THE CORRUPTION TO BE FOUND IN SOLITUDE. WE HAVE TORN OURSELVES FROM THE TRUTH WHICH IS OUR BROTHER MEN... THERE IS NO ROAD BACK FOR US, AND NO REDEMPTION...
WE KNOW THESE THINGS BUT WE DO NOT CARE. WE CARE FOR NOTHING ON EARTH... WE ARE TIRED.
ONLY THE GLASS BOX IN OUR ARMS IS LIKE A LIVING HEART THAT GIVES STRENGTH.
WE HAVE LIED TO OURSELVES. WE HAVE NOT BUILT THIS BOX FOR THE GOOD OF OUR BROTHERS. WE BUILT IT FOR ITS OWN SAKE. IT IS ABOVE ALL OUR BROTHERS TO US---ITS TRUTH ABOVE THEIR TRUTH.
WHY WONDER THIS? WE HAVE NOT MANY DAYS TO LIVE. WE ARE WALKING TO THE FANGS AWAITING US SOMEWHERE AMONG THE GREAT SILENT TREES. THERE IS NOT A THING BEHIND US TO REGRET.
THEN A BLOW OF PAIN STRUCK US--OUR FIRST AND ONLY... WE THOUGHT OF THE GOLDEN ONE.
WE THOUGHT OF THE GOLDEN ONE WHOM WE SHALL NEVER SEE AGAIN.
THEN THE PAIN PASSED. IT IS BEST...
WE ARE ONE OF THE DAMNED... IT IS BEST IF THE GOLDEN ONE FORGOT OUR NAME...
AND FORGOT THE BODY WHICH BORE THAT NAME.

WE HAVE NOT WRITTEN FOR MANY DAYS. WE DID NOT WISH TO SPEAK. FOR WE NEEDED NO WORDS TO REMEMBER THAT WHICH HAS HAPPENED TO US.
IT WAS ON OUR SECOND DAY IN THE FOREST THAT WE HEARD STEPS BEHIND US.
WE HID IN THE BUSHES, AND WE WAITED... THE STEPS CAME CLOSER.
AND WE SAW THE FOLD OF A WHITE TUNIC AMONG THE TREES AND A GLEAM OF GOLD.
THEY SAW US. AND THEIR HANDS CLOSED INTO FISTS AND THE FISTS PULLED THEIR ARMS DOWN --AS IF THEY WISHED THEIR ARMS TO HOLD THEM...WHILE THEIR BODY SWAYED.
WE LEPT FORWARD! WE RAN TO THEM-- AND WE STOOD LOOKING UPON THE GOLDEN ONE.
AND THEY COULD NOT SPEAK.
WE DARED NOT COME TOO CLOSE TO THEM.... WE ASKED AND OUR VOICE TREMBLED:
HOW COME YOU TO BE HERE, GOLDEN ONE?
BUT THEY WHISPERED ONLY:
WE HAVE FOUND YOU...
HOW COME YOU TO BE IN THE FOREST?
THEY RAISED THEIR HEAD...AND THERE WAS GREAT PRIDE IN THEIR VOICE; THEY ANSWERED:
WE HAVE FOLLOWED YOU.

WE SAT STILL AND WE HELD OUR BREATH--FOR OUR FACE AND OUR BODY WERE BEAUTIFUL. OUR FACE WAS NOT LIKE THE FACES OF OUR BROTHERS, FOR WE FELT NO PITY WHEN LOOKING UPON IT.
OUR BODY WAS NOT LIKE THE BODIES OF OUR BROTHERS... FOR OUR LIMBS WERE STRAIGHT AND THIN AND HARD AND STRONG.
AND WE THOUGHT THAT WE COULD TRUST THIS BEING WHO LOOKED UPON US FROM THE STREAM, AND THAT WE HAD NOTHING TO FEAR WITH THIS BEING.
WE WALKED ON TILL THE SUN HAD SET.
WHEN THE SHADOWS GATHERED AMONG THE TREES, WE STOPPED IN A HOLLOW BETWEEN THE ROOTS WHERE WE SHALL SLEEP TONIGHT.
AND SUDDENLY-- FOR THE FIRST TIME THIS DAY, WE REMEMBERED THAT WE ARE THE DAMNED... WE REMEMBERED IT, AND WE LAUGHED.
WE ARE WRITING THIS ON THE PAPER WE HAD HIDDEN IN OUR TUNIC, TOGETHER WITH THE WRITTEN PAGES WE HAD BROUGHT FOR THE WORLD COUNCIL OF SCHOLARS BUT NEVER GIVEN TO THEM.
WE HAVE MUCH TO SPEAK OF TO OURSELVES...
...WE HOPE WE SHALL FIND THE WORDS FOR IT IN THE DAYS TO COME.
NOW, WE CANNOT SPEAK, FOR WE CANNOT UNDERSTAND.

THEN WE TOOK OUR GLASS BOX AND WE WENT ON INTO THE FOREST.
WE WENT ON...CUTTING THROUGH THE BRANCHES AS IF WE WERE SWIMMING THROUGH A SEA OF LEAVES... WITH THE BUSHES AS WAVES, RISING AND FALLING AROUND US.
THE TREES PARTED BEFORE US-- CALLING US FORWARD. THE FOREST SEEMED TO WELCOME US. WE WENT ON, WITHOUT CARE, WITH NOTHING TO FEEL-- SAVE THE SONG OF OUR BODY.
WE STOPPED WHEN WE FELT HUNGER.
WE SAW BIRDS IN THE TREE BRANCHES, AND FLYING FROM UNDER OUR FOOTSTEPS.
WE PICKED UP A STONE AND WE SENT IT AS AN ARROW AT A BIRD.
IT FELL BEFORE US. WE MADE FIRE, WE COOKED THE BIRD AND WE ATE IT. NO OTHER MEAL HAD EVER TASTED BETTER TO US.
AND WE THOUGHT SUDDENLY, THAT THERE WAS A GREAT SATISFACTION TO BE FOUND IN THE FOOD WHICH WE NEED AND OBTAIN BY OUR OWN HAND.
AND WE WISHED TO BE HUNGRY AGAIN, AND SOON, THAT WE MIGHT KNOW AGAIN, THIS STRANGE NEW PRIDE IN EATING.
THEN WE WALKED ON...
AND WE CAME TO A STREAM WHICH LAY AS A STREAK OF GLASS AMONG THE TREES.
IT LAY SO STILL THAT WE SAW NO WATER, BUT ONLY A CUT IN THE EARTH... IN WHICH THE TREES GREW DOWN, UPTURNED AND THE SKY LAY AT THE BOTTOM.
WE KNELT BY THE STREAM AND WE BENT DOWN TO DRINK AND THEN WE STOPPED...
FOR UPON THE BLUE OF THE SKY BELOW US, WE SAW OUR OWN FACE FOR THE FIRST TIME.

IT HAS BEEN A DAY OF WONDER... THIS OUR FIRST DAY IN THE FOREST.
WE AWOKE WHEN A RAY OF SUNLIGHT FELL ACROSS OUR FACE. WE WANTED TO LEAP TO OUR FEET, AS WE HAVE TO LEAP EVERY MORNING OF OUR LIFE, BUT WE REMEMBERED SUDDENLY THAT THERE WAS NO BELL TO RING ANYWHERE.
WE DID NOT WISH TO MOVE. WE THOUGHT SUDDENLY, THAT WE COULD LIE THUS AS LONG AS WE WISHED--WE COULD ALSO RISE, OR RUN, OR LEAP, OR FALL DOWN AGAIN.
BEFORE WE KNEW IT OUR BODY HAD RISEN IN ONE LEAP... OUR ARMS STRETCHED OUT OF THEIR OWN WILL. OUR HANDS SEIZED A BRANCH AND SWUNG US HIGH INTO A TREE, WITH NO AIM SAVE THE WONDER OF LEARNING THE STRENGTH OF OUR BODY.
THE BRANCH SNAPPED UNDER US!
OUR BODY, LOSING ALL SENSE, ROLLED OVER AND OVER ON THE MOSS... DRY LEAVES IN OUR TUNIC, IN OUR HAIR, IN OUR FACE.
AND WE HEARD SUDDENLY THAT WE WERE LAUGHING.
LAUGHING ALOUD, LAUGHING AS IF THERE WERE NO POWER LEFT IN US SAVE LAUGHTER.

WE HEARD THAT YOU HAD GONE TO THE UNCHARTED FOREST--FOR THE WHOLE CITY IS SPEAKING OF IT. SO ON THE NIGHT OF THE DAY WHEN WE HEARD IT, WE RAN AWAY FROM THE HOME OF THE PEASANTS.
WE FOUND THE MARKS OF YOUR FEET ACROSS THE PLAIN WHERE NO MEN WALK. SO WE FOLLOWED THEM, AND WE WENT INTO THE FOREST, AND WE FOLLOWED THE PATH WHERE THE BRANCHES WERE BROKEN BY YOUR BODY.
THEIR WHITE TUNIC WAS TORN AND THE BRANCHES HAD CUT THE SKIN OF THEIR ARMS...BUT THEY SPOKE AS IF THEY HAD NEVER TAKEN NOTICE OF IT-- NOR OF THEIR WEARINESS, NOR OF FEAR.
WE HAVE FOLLOWED YOU, AND WE SHALL FOLLOW YOU WHEREVER YOU GO.
IF DANGER THREATENS YOU, WE SHALL FACE IT ALSO. IF IT BE DEATH, WE SHALL DIE WITH YOU.
YOU ARE DAMNED AND WE WISH TO SHARE YOUR DAMNATION.
YOUR EYES ARE AS A FLAME... BUT OUR BROTHERS HAVE NEITHER HOPE NOR FIRE.
YOUR MOUTH IS CUT OF GRANITE... BUT OUR BROTHERS ARE SOFT AND HUMBLE. YOUR HEAD IS HIGH, BUT OUR BROTHERS CRINGE.
WE WISH TO BE DAMNED WITH YOU-- RATHER THAN BE BLESSED WITH ALL OUR BROTHERS. DO AS YOU PLEASE WITH US...BUT DO NOT SEND US AWAY FROM YOU.
WE HAD NEVER THOUGHT OF THAT WHICH WE DID.
WE BENT TO RAISE THE GOLDEN ONE TO THEIR FEET...BUT WHEN WE TOUCHED THEM, IT WAS AS IF MADNESS HAD STRICKEN US. WE SEIZED THEIR BODY AND PRESSED OUR LIPS TO THEIRS.
THE GOLDEN ONE BREATHED ONCE... AND THEIR BREATH WAS A MOAN, AND THEN THEIR ARMS CLOSED AROUND US.

WE STOOD TOGETHER FOR A LONG TIME--AND WE WERE FRIGHTENED THAT WE HAD LIVED FOR TWENTY-ONE YEARS AND HAD NEVER KNOWN WHAT JOY IS POSSIBLE TO MEN.
THEN WE SAID:
OUR DEAREST ONE, FEAR NOTHING OF THE FOREST. THERE IS NO DANGER IN SOLITUDE. WE HAVE NO NEED OF OUR BROTHERS. LET US FORGET THEIR GOOD AND OUR EVIL. LET US FORGET ALL THINGS SAVE THAT WE ARE TOGETHER AND THAT THERE IS JOY AS A BOND BETWEEN US.
LOOK AHEAD. IT IS OUR OWN WORLD, GOLDEN ONE-- A STRANGE UNKNOWN WORLD... BUT OUR OWN.
THEN WE WALKED ON INTO THE FOREST, THEIR HANDS IN OURS.
AND THAT NIGHT WE KNEW THAT TO HOLD THE BODY OF WOMAN IN OUR ARMS IS NEITHER UGLY NOR SHAMEFUL, BUT THE ONE ECSTASY GRANTED TO THE RACE OF MEN.

WE HAVE WALKED FOR MANY DAYS.
THE FOREST HAS NO END, AND WE SEEK NO END.
BUT EACH DAY ADDED TO THE CHAIN OF DAYS BETWEEN US AND THE CITY IS LIKE AN ADDED BLESSING.
WE HAVE MADE A BOW AND MANY ARROWS. WE CAN KILL MORE THAN WE NEED FOR OUR FOOD.
WE FIND WATER AND FRUIT IN THE FOREST.
AT NIGHT, WE CHOOSE A CLEARING... AND WE BUILD A RING OF FIRES AROUND IT.
WE SLEEP IN THE MIDST OF THAT RING-- THE BEASTS DARE NOT ATTACK US.
WE CAN SEE THEIR EYES, GREEN AND YELLOW AS COALS, WATCHING US FROM THE TREE BRANCHES BEYOND.
THE FIRES SMOLDER AS A CROWN OF JEWELS AROUND US--AND SMOKE STANDS STILL IN THE AIR IN COLUMNS MADE BLUE BY THE MOONLIGHT.
WE SLEEP TOGETHER IN THE MIDST OF THE RING... THE ARMS OF THE GOLDEN ONE AROUND US...THEIR HEAD UPON OUR BREAST.

SOME DAY WE SHALL STOP AND BUILD A HOUSE... WHEN WE SHALL HAVE GONE FAR ENOUGH.
BUT WE DO NOT HAVE TO HASTEN.
THE DAYS BEFORE US ARE WITHOUT END. LIKE THE FOREST.
WE CANNOT UNDERSTAND THIS NEW LIFE WHICH WE HAVE FOUND. YET IT SEEMS SO CLEAR AND SO SIMPLE.
WHEN QUESTIONS COME TO PUZZLE US... WE WALK FASTER--THEN TURN AND FORGET ALL THINGS AS WE WATCH THE GOLDEN ONE FOLLOWING.
THEY APPROACH US... AND THEY STOP--LAUGHING, KNOWING WHAT WE THINK...
WE GO ON...
BUT QUESTIONS COME TO US AGAIN, AS WE WALK IN SILENCE. IF THIS IS THE GREAT EVIL OF BEING ALONE...
THEN WHAT IS GOOD... AND WHAT IS EVIL?
EVERYTHING WHICH COMES FROM MANY IS GOOD... EVERTHING WHICH COMES FROM ONE IS EVIL.
THUS HAVE WE BEEN TAUGHT WITH OUR FIRST BREATH. WE HAVE BROKEN THE LAW-- BUT WE HAVE NEVER DOUBTED IT.
YET NOW-- AS WE WALK THROUGH THE FOREST ... WE ARE LEARNING TO DOUBT.

THERE IS NO LIFE FOR MEN-- SAVE IN USEFUL TOIL FOR THE GOOD OF ALL OUR BROTHERS. BUT WHEN WE TOILED FOR OUR BROTHERS, WE WERE ONLY WEARY.
BUT THE ONLY THINGS WHICH TAUGHT US JOY WERE THE POWER WE CREATED IN OUR WIRES AND THE GOLDEN ONE.
AND BOTH THESE JOYS BELONG TO US ALONE.
THUS DO WE WONDER.
THERE IS SOME ERROR-- ONE FRIGHTFUL ERROR, IN THE THINKING OF MEN... WHAT IS THAT ERROR?
WE DO NOT KNOW, BUT THE KNOWLEDGE STRUGGLES WITHIN US, STRUGGLES TO BE BORN.
TODAY THE GOLDEN ONE STOPPED SUDDENLY AND SAID:
WE LOVE YOU.
BUT THEN THEY FROWNED AND SHOOK THEIR HEAD, AND LOOKED AT US HELPLESSLY.
NO, THAT IS NOT WHAT WE WISHED TO SAY.
THEY WERE SILENT--THEN THEY SPOKE SLOWLY...AND THEIR WORDS WERE HALTING...
WE ARE ONE... ALONE... AND ONLY... AND WE LOVE YOU WHO ARE ONE... ALONE... AND ONLY.
WE LOOKED INTO EACH OTHER'S EYES AND WE KNEW THAT THE BREATH OF A MIRACLE HAD TOUCHED US AND FLED AND LEFT US GROPING VAINLY.
AND WE FELT TORN---- TORN FOR SOME WORD WE COULD NOT FIND.

WE ARE SITTING AT A TABLE, AND WE ARE WRITING THIS UPON PAPER MADE THOUSANDS OF YEARS AGO.
THE LIGHT IS DIM... AND WE CANNOT SEE THE GOLDEN ONE...
ONLY A LOCK OF GOLD ON THE PILLOW OF THE ANCIENT BED. THIS IS OUR HOME.
WE CAME UPON IT TODAY AT SUNRISE...
FOR MANY DAYS WE HAD BEEN CROSSING A CHAIN OF MOUNTAINS.
THE FOREST ROSE AMONG THE CLIFFS, AND WHENEVER WE WALKED OUT UPON A BARREN STRETCH OF ROCK, WE SAW GREAT PEAKS BEFORE US IN THE WEST, AND TO THE NORTH OF US, AND TO THE SOUTH...AS FAR AS OUR EYES COULD SEE.
WE HAD NEVER HEARD OF THESE MOUNTAINS-- NOR SEEN THEM MARKED ON ANY MAP. THE UNCHARTED FOREST HAS PROTECTED THEM FROM THE CITIES... AND FROM THE MEN OF THE CITIES.
WE CLIMBED PATHS WHERE THE WILD GOAT DARED NOT FOLLOW.
STONES ROLLED FROM UNDER OUR FEET...AND WE HEARD THEM STRIKING THE ROCKS BELOW...FARTHER AND FARTHER DOWN-- AND THE MOUNTAINS RANG WITH EACH STROKE.
BUT WE WENT ON... FOR WE KNEW THAT NO MEN WOULD EVER FOLLOW OUR TRACKS NOR REACH US HERE.
THEN WE SAW A WHITE FLAME AMONG THE TREES-- HIGH ON A SHEER PEAK BEFORE US.
WE THOUGHT THAT IT WAS FIRE, AND WE STOPPED. BUT THE FLAME WAS UNMOVING-- YET BLINDING AS LIQUID METAL.
SO WE CLIMBED TOWARD IT-- AND THERE, BEFORE US...ON A BROAD SUMMIT... WITH THE MOUNTAINS RISING BEHIND IT, STOOD A HOUSE SUCH AS WE HAD NEVER SEEN... AND THE WHITE FIRE CAME FROM THE SUN ON THE GLASS OF ITS WINDOWS.

THE HOUSE HAD TWO STORIES AND A STRANGE ROOF FLAT AS A FLOOR. THERE WAS MORE WINDOW THAN WALL UPON ITS WALLS...AND THE WINDOWS WENT ON STRAIGHT AROUND THE CORNERS, THOUGH HOW THIS KEPT THE HOUSE STANDING WE COULD NOT GUESS.
THE WALLS WERE HARD AND SMOOTH, OF THAT STONE--UNLIKE STONE--WHICH WE HAD SEEN IN OUR TUNNEL.
WE BOTH KNEW IT WITHOUT WORDS: THIS HOUSE WAS LEFT FROM THE UNMENTIONABLE TIMES...
THE TREES HAD PROTECTED IT FROM TIME AND WEATHER ...AND FROM MEN WHO HAVE LESS PITY THAN TIME AND WEATHER.
WE TURNED TO THE GOLDEN ONE AND WE ASKED:
ARE YOU AFRAID?
BUT THEY SHOOK THEIR HEAD.
SO WE WALKED TO THE DOOR AND WE THREW IT OPEN--AND WE STEPPED TOGETHER INTO THE HOUSE OF THE UNMENTIONABLE TIMES.
WE SHALL NEED THE DAYS AND THE YEARS AHEAD TO LOOK--TO LEARN AND TO UNDERSTAND THE THINGS OF THIS HOUSE. TODAY, WE COULD ONLY LOOK AND TRY TO BELIEVE THE SIGHT OF OUR EYES.
NEVER HAD WE SEEN ROOMS SO FULL OF LIGHT.
THE SUNRAYS DANCED UPON COLORS...
...MORE COLORS THAN WE THOUGHT POSSIBLE--WE WHO HAD SEEN NO HOUSES SAVE THE WHITE ONES THE BROWN ONES AND THE GREY.
THERE WERE GREAT PIECES OF GLASS ON THE WALLS--BUT IT WAS NOT GLASS...
FOR WHEN WE LOOKED UPON IT, WE SAW OUR OWN BODIES AND ALL THE THINGS BEHIND US, AS ON THE FACE OF A LAKE. THERE WERE STRANGE THINGS WHICH WE HAD NEVER SEEN AND THE USE OF WHICH WE DO NOT KNOW.... AND THERE WERE GLOBES OF GLASS EVERYWHERE... THE GLOBES WITH THE METAL COBWEBS INSIDE--SUCH AS WE HAD SEEN IN OUR TUNNEL.

WE FOUND THE SLEEPING HALL AND WE STOOD IN AWE UPON ITS THRESHOLD.
WE FOUND NO OTHER BEDS IN THE HOUSE AND THEN WE KNEW THAT ONLY TWO PEOPLE HAD LIVED HERE--AND THIS PASSES UNDERSTANDING....WHAT KIND OF WORLD DID THEY HAVE IN THE UNMENTIONABLE TIMES?
WE FOUND GARMENTS AND THE GOLDEN ONE GASPED AT THE SIGHT OF THEM.
FOR THEY WERE NOT WHITE TUNICS, NOR WHITE TOGAS; THEY WERE OF ALL COLORS, NO TWO OF THEM ALIKE, SOME CRUMBLED TO DUST AS WE TOUCHED THEM.
BUT OTHERS WERE OF HEAVIER CLOTH, AND THEY FELT SOFT AND NEW IN OUR FINGERS.
WE FOUND A ROOM WITH WALLS MADE OF SHELVES... WHICH HELD ROWS OF MANUSCRIPTS, FROM THE FLOOR TO THE CEILING... NEVER HAD WE SEEN SUCH A NUMBER OF THEM--NOR OF SUCH STRANGE SHAPE. THEY WERE NOT SOFT AND ROLLED--THEY HAD HARD SHELLS OF CLOTH AND LEATHER.
LETTERS ON THE PAGES WERE SO SMALL AND SO EVEN THAT WE WONDERED AT THE MEN WHO HAD SUCH HANDWRITING. WE GLANCED THROUGH THE PAGES--AND WE SAW THAT THEY WERE WRITTEN IN OUR LANGUAGE--BUT WE FOUND MANY WORDS WHICH WE COULD NOT UNDERSTAND.
TOMORROW WE SHALL BEGIN TO READ THESE SCRIPTS.
WHEN WE HAD SEEN ALL THE ROOMS OF THE HOUSE WE LOOKED AT THE GOLDEN ONE AND WE BOTH KNEW THE THOUGHT IN OUR MINDS.
WE SHALL NEVER LEAVE THIS HOUSE, NOR LET IT BE TAKEN FROM US. THIS IS OUR HOME AND THE END OF OUR JOURNEY.
--THIS IS YOUR HOUSE, GOLDEN ONE--AND OURS. WE SHALL NOT SHARE IT WITH OTHERS, AS WE SHARE NOT OUR JOY WITH THEM, NOR OUR LOVE, NOR OUR HUNGER. SO BE IT TO THE END OF OUR DAYS.
YOUR WILL BE DONE.

THEN WE WENT OUT TO GATHER WOOD FOR THE GREAT HEARTH OF OUR HOME.
WE BROUGHT WATER FROM THE STREAM WHICH RUNS AMONG THE TREES UNDER OUR WINDOWS...
WE KILLED A MOUNTAIN GOAT.
WE BROUGHT ITS FLESH TO BE COOKED IN A STRANGE COPPER POT WE FOUND IN A PLACE OF WONDERS... WHICH MUST HAVE BEEN THE COOKING ROOM OF THE HOUSE.
WE DID THIS WORK ALONE...
...NO WORDS OF OURS COULD TAKE THE GOLDEN ONE AWAY FROM THE BIG GLASS WHICH IS NOT GLASS--THEY STOOD BEFORE IT AND THEY LOOKED AND LOOKED UPON THEIR OWN BODY.
WHEN THE SUN SANK BEYOND THE MOUNTAINS, THE GOLDEN ONE FELL ASLEEP ON THE FLOOR... AMIDST JEWELS AND BOTTLES OF CRYSTAL AND FLOWERS OF SILK. WE LIFTED THE GOLDEN ONE IN OUR ARMS AND WE CARRIED THEM TO A BED...THEIR HEAD FALLING SOFTLY UPON OUR SHOULDER.
THEN WE LIT A CANDLE AND WE BROUGHT PAPER FROM THE ROOM OF THE MANUSCRIPTS... AND WE SAT BY THE WINDOW...
...FOR WE KNEW THAT WE COULD NOT SLEEP TONIGHT.

AND NOW WE LOOK UPON THE EARTH AND SKY.
THIS SPREAD OF NAKED ROCK AND PEAKS, AND MOONLIGHT IS LIKE A WORLD READY TO BE BORN-- A WORLD THAT WAITS.
IT SEEMS TO US IT ASKS A SIGN FROM US--A SPARK, A FIRST COMMANDMENT. WE CANNOT KNOW WHAT WORD WE ARE TO GIVE-- NOR WHAT GREAT DEED THIS EARTH EXPECTS TO WITNESS.
WE KNOW IT WAITS... IT SEEMS TO SAY IT HAS GREAT GIFTS TO LAY BEFORE US, BUT IT WISHED A GREATER GIFT FROM US. WE ARE TO SPEAK. WE ARE TO GIVE ITS GOAL, ITS HIGHEST MEANING TO ALL THIS GLOWING SPACE OF ROCK AND SKY.
WE LOOK AHEAD-- WE BEG OUR HEART FOR GUIDANCE IN ANSWERING THIS CALL NO VOICE HAS SPOKEN...YET WE HAVE HEARD. WE LOOK UPON OUR HANDS. WE SEE DUST OF CENTURIES--THE DUST WHICH HID GREAT SECRETS, AND PERHAPS GREAT EVILS... AND YET IT STIRS NO FEAR WITHIN OUR HEART, BUT ONLY SILENT REVERENCE AND PITY.
MAY KNOWLEDGE COME TO US! WHAT IS THE SECRET OUR HEART HAS UNDERSTOOD, AND YET WILL NOT REVEAL TO US...ALTHOUGH IT SEEMS TO BEAT AS IF IT WERE ENDEAVORING TO TELL IT?

I AM.
I THINK.
I WILL.
MY HANDS... MY SPIRIT... MY FOREST...
THIS EARTH OF MINE...
WHAT MUST I SAY BESIDES? THESE ARE THE WORDS.
THIS IS THE ANSWER.
I STAND HERE ON THE SUMMIT OF THE MOUNTAIN.
I LIFT MY HEAD AND I SPREAD MY ARMS.
THIS-- MY BODY AND SPIRIT...THIS IS THE END OF THE QUEST.
I WISHED TO KNOW THE MEANING OF THINGS... I AM THE MEANING. I WISHED TO FIND A WARRANT FOR BEING--AND NO WORD OF SANCTION UPON MY BEING.
I AM THE WARRANT AND THE SANCTION.
IT IS MY EYES WHICH SEE, AND THE SIGHT OF MY EYES GRANTS BEAUTY TO THE EARTH.
IT IS MY EARS WHICH HEAR... AND THE HEARING OF MY EARS GIVES ITS SONG TO THE WORLD.
IT IS MY MIND WHICH THINKS-- AND THE JUDGEMENT OF MY MIND IS THE ONLY SEARCHLIGHT THAT CAN FIND THE TRUTH. IT IS MY WILL WHICH CHOOSES... AND THE CHOICE OF MY WILL IS THE ONLY EDICT I MUST RESPECT.

MANY WORDS HAVE BEEN GRANTED ME...SOME ARE WISE...SOME ARE FALSE...
BUT ONLY THREE ARE HOLY...
I... WILL... IT!
WHATEVER ROAD I TAKE... THE GUIDING STAR IS WITHIN ME; THE GUIDING STAR AND THE LOADSTONE WHICH POINT THE WAY-- THEY POINT IN ONE DIRECTION. THEY POINT TO ME.
I KNOW NOT IF THIS EARTH ON WHICH I STAND IS THE CORE OF THE UNIVERSE, OR IF IT IS BUT A SPECK OF DUST LOST IN ETERNITY.
I KNOW NOT AND CARE NOT... FOR I KNOW WHAT HAPPINESS IS POSSIBLE TO ME ON EARTH.
AND MY HAPPINESS NEEDS NO HIGHER AIM TO VINDICATE IT...MY HAPPINESS IS NOT THE MEANS TO ANY END... IT IS THE END.
IT IS ITS OWN GOAL. IT IS ITS OWN PURPOSE.
NEITHER AM I THE MEANS TO ANY END OTHERS MAY WISH TO ACCOMPLISH... I AM NOT A TOOL FOR THEIR USE. I AM NOT A SERVANT OF THEIR NEEDS-- I AM NOT A BANDAGE FOR THEIR WOUNDS.
I AM NOT A SACRIFICE ON THEIR ALTARS.
I AM A MAN.
THIS MIRACLE OF ME IS MINE TO OWN, AND KEEP... MINE TO GUARD...AND MINE TO USE --AND MINE TO KNEEL BEFORE!

E" MUST NEVER BY ONE'S CHOICE THOUGHT.
NEVER BE PLACED N'S SOUL...ELSE IT STER...
...THE ROOT OF ALL EVILS ON EARTH ...THE ROOT OF MAN'S TORTURE BY MEN--AND OF AN UNSPEAKABLE LIE.
THE WORD "WE" IS AS LIME POURED OVER MEN... WHICH SETS AND HARDENS TO STONE AND CRUSHES ALL BENEATH IT...AND THAT WHICH IS WHITE AND THAT IS BLACK ARE LOST EQUALLY IN THE GREY OF IT.
IT IS A WORD BY WHICH THE DEPRAVED STEAL THE VIRTUE OF THE GOOD--BY WHICH THE WEAK STEAL THE MIGHT OF THE STRONG...BY WHICH FOOLS STEAL THE WISDOM OF SAGES.
WHAT IS MY JOY IF ALL HANDS, EVEN THE UNCLEAN, CAN REACH INTO IT?! WHAT IS MY WISDOM, IF EVEN FOOLS CAN DICTATE TO ME?!
WHAT IS MY FREEDOM IF ALL CREATURES EVEN THE BOTCHED AND IMPOTENT ARE MY MASTERS?!
WHAT IS MY LIFE IF I AM TO BOW, TO AGREE ...TO OBEY?!
AM DONE WITH THIS CREED OF CORRUPTION.
I AM DONE WITH THE MONSTER OF "WE" ...THE WORD OF SERFDOM--OF PLUNDER, OF MISERY... OF FALSEHOOD AND SHAME.
AND NOW I SEE THE FACE OF GOD...AND I RAISE THIS GOD OVER THE EARTH--THIS GOD WHOM MEN HAVE SOUGHT SINCE MEN CAME INTO BEING...THIS GOD WHO WILL GRANT THEM JOY AND PEACE AND PRIDE.
THIS GOD...THIS ONE WORD.
"I."

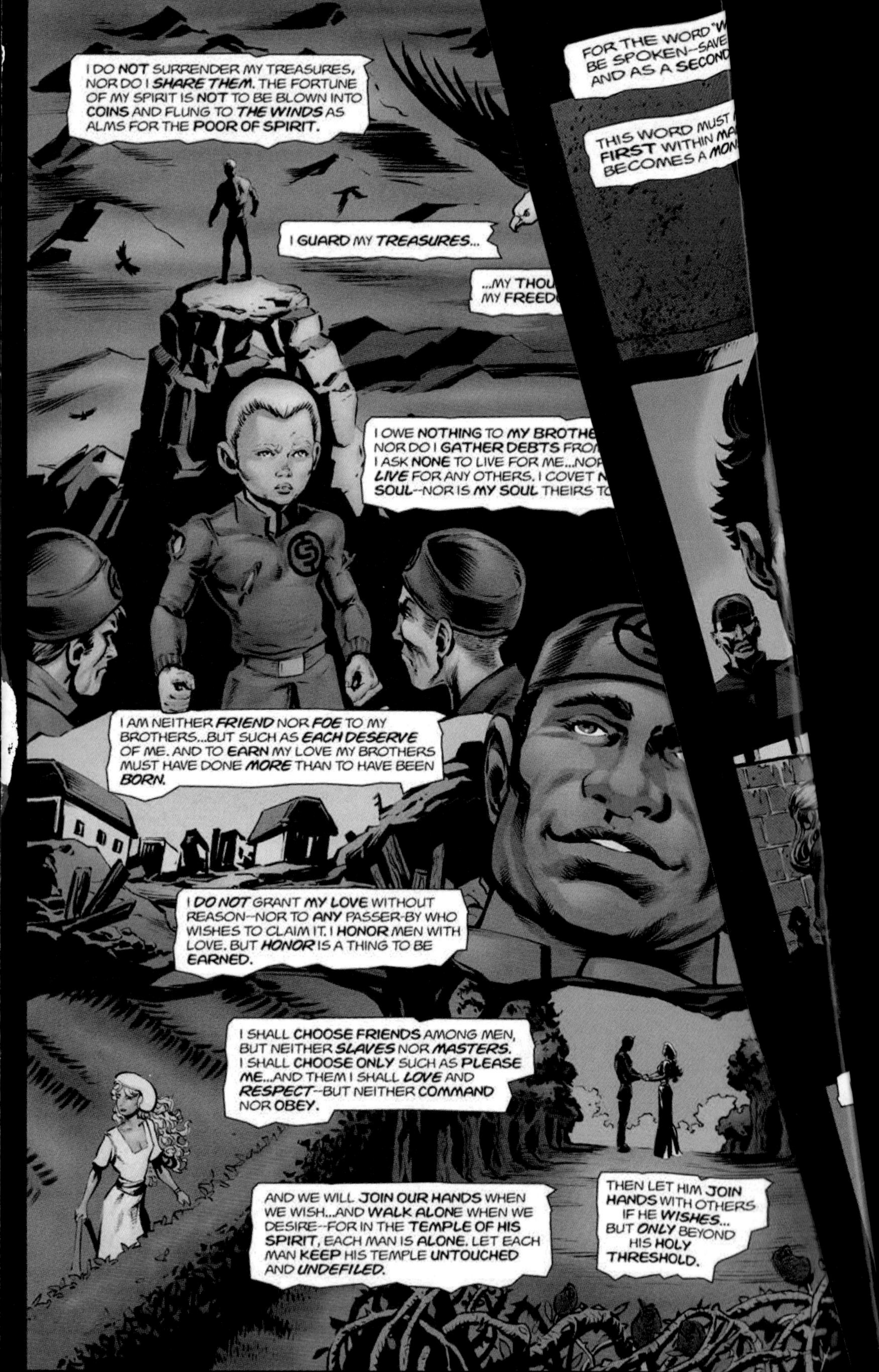
I DO NOT SURRENDER MY TREASURES, NOR DO I SHARE THEM. THE FORTUNE OF MY SPIRIT IS NOT TO BE BLOWN INTO COINS AND FLUNG TO THE WINDS AS ALMS FOR THE POOR OF SPIRIT.
I GUARD MY TREASURES...
...MY THOU
MY FREED
I OWE NOTHING TO MY BROTHE
NOR DO I GATHER DEBTS FROM
I ASK NONE TO LIVE FOR ME...NOR
LIVE FOR ANY OTHERS. I COVET N
SOUL--NOR IS MY SOUL THEIRS TO
I AM NEITHER FRIEND NOR FOE TO MY BROTHERS...BUT SUCH AS EACH DESERVE OF ME. AND TO EARN MY LOVE MY BROTHERS MUST HAVE DONE MORE THAN TO HAVE BEEN BORN.
I DO NOT GRANT MY LOVE WITHOUT REASON--NOR TO ANY PASSER-BY WHO WISHES TO CLAIM IT. I HONOR MEN WITH LOVE. BUT HONOR IS A THING TO BE EARNED.
I SHALL CHOOSE FRIENDS AMONG MEN, BUT NEITHER SLAVES NOR MASTERS. I SHALL CHOOSE ONLY SUCH AS PLEASE ME...AND THEM I SHALL LOVE AND RESPECT--BUT NEITHER COMMAND NOR OBEY.
AND WE WILL JOIN OUR HANDS WHEN WE WISH...AND WALK ALONE WHEN WE DESIRE--FOR IN THE TEMPLE OF HIS SPIRIT, EACH MAN IS ALONE. LET EACH MAN KEEP HIS TEMPLE UNTOUCHED AND UNDEFILED.
THEN LET HIM JOIN HANDS WITH OTHERS IF HE WISHES... BUT ONLY BEYOND HIS HOLY THRESHOLD.
FOR THE WORD "W
BE SPOKEN--SAVE
AND AS A SECOND
THIS WORD MUST
FIRST WITHIN MA
BECOMES A MON

IT WAS WHEN I READ THE FIRST OF THE BOOKS I FOUND IN MY HOUSE THAT I SAW THE WORD "I." AND WHEN I UNDERSTOOD THIS WORD... THE BOOK FELL FROM MY HANDS...AND I WEPT...I WHO HAD NEVER KNOWN TEARS.
I WEPT IN DELIVERANCE, AND IN PITY FOR ALL MANKIND.
I UNDERSTOOD THE BLESSED THING THAT I CALLED MY CURSE. I UNDERSTOOD WHY THE BEST IN ME HAD BEEN MY SINS AND MY TRANSGRESSIONS; AND WHY I HAD NEVER FELT GUILT IN MY SINS....I UNDERSTOOD THAT CENTURIES OF CHAINS AND LASHES WILL NOT KILL THE SPIRIT OF MAN NOR THE SENSE OF TRUTH WITHIN HIM.
I READ MANY BOOKS FOR MANY DAYS. THEN I CALLED THE GOLDEN ONE... AND I TOLD HER WHAT I HAD READ AND WHAT I HAD LEARNED...
SHE LOOKED AT ME, AND THE FIRST WORDS SHE SPOKE WERE:
I LOVE YOU.
MY DEAREST ONE, IT IS NOT PROPER FOR MEN TO BE WITHOUT NAMES. THERE WAS A TIME WHEN EACH MAN HAD A NAME OF HIS OWN TO DISTINGUISH HIM FROM ALL OTHER MEN. SO LET US CHOOSE OUR NAMES. I HAVE READ OF A MAN WHO LIVED MANY THOUSANDS OF YEARS AGO...AND OF ALL THE NAMES IN THESE BOOKS, HIS IS THE ONE I WISH TO BEAR. HE TOOK THE LIGHT OF THE GODS AND HE BROUGHT IT TO MEN--AND HE TAUGHT MEN TO BE GODS. AND HE SUFFERED FOR THIS DEED, AS ALL BEARERS OF LIGHT MUST SUFFER. HIS NAME WAS "PROMETHEUS."
IT SHALL BE YOUR NAME.
AND I HAVE READ OF A GODDESS--WHO WAS MOTHER OF THE EARTH, AND OF ALL THE GODS. HER NAME WAS "GAEA." LET THIS BE YOUR NAME...FOR YOU ARE TO BE THE MOTHER OF A NEW KIND OF GODS.
IT SHALL BE MY NAME.

NOW I LOOK AHEAD...
MY FUTURE IS CLEAR BEFORE ME...
THE SAINT OF THE PYRE HAD SEEN THE FUTURE WHEN HE CHOSE ME AS HIS HEIR--AS HEIR OF ALL THE SAINTS AND ALL THE MARTYRS WHO CAME BEFORE HIM, AND WHO DIED FOR THE SAME CAUSE...FOR THE SAME WORD...NO MATTER WHAT NAME THEY GAVE TO THEIR CAUSE AND THEIR TRUTH.
I SHALL LIVE HERE IN MY OWN HOUSE...I SHALL TAKE MY FOOD FROM THE EARTH BY TOIL OF MY OWN HANDS.
THROUGH THE YEARS AHEAD I SHALL REBUILD THE ACHIEVEMENTS OF THE PAST...AND OPEN THE WAY TO CARRY THEM FURTHER...
...THE ACHIEVEMENTS WHICH ARE OPEN TO ME-- BUT CLOSED FOREVER TO MY BROTHERS... FOR THEIR MINDS ARE SHACKLED TO THE WEAKEST AND DULLEST ONES AMONG THEM.

I HAVE LEARNED THAT MY POWER OF THE SKY WAS KNOWN TO MEN LONG AGO...
...THEY CALLED IT ELECTRICITY.
IT WAS THE POWER THAT MOVED THEIR GREATEST INVENTIONS...
IT LIT THIS HOUSE WITH LIGHT WHICH CAME FROM THOSE GLOBES OF GLASS ON THE WALLS...
I HAVE FOUND THE ENGINE WHICH PRODUCED THIS LIGHT...
I SHALL REPAIR IT...AND LEARN HOW TO MAKE IT WORK AGAIN.
I SHALL LEARN HOW TO USE THE WIRES THAT CARRY THE POWER...
THEN I SHALL BUILD A BARRIER OF WIRES AROUND MY HOME... AND ACROSS THE PATHS WHICH LEAD TO MY HOME...
A BARRIER AS LIGHT AS A COBWEB...MORE IMPASSABLE THAN A WALL OF GRANITE...

...A BARRIER MY BROTHERS WILL NEVER BE ABLE TO CROSS...
FOR THEY HAVE NOTHING TO FIGHT ME WITH--SAVE THE BRUTE FORCE OF THEIR NUMBERS...
I HAVE MY MIND.
THEN HERE...ON THIS MOUNTAINTOP...WITH THE WORLD BELOW ME AND NOTHING ABOVE ME BUT THE SUN--I SHALL LIVE MY OWN TRUTH.
GAEA IS PREGNANT WITH MY CHILD.
OUR SON WILL BE RAISED AS A MAN... HE WILL BE TAUGHT TO SAY "I" AND TO BEAR THE PRIDE OF IT.
HE WILL BE TAUGHT TO WALK STRAIGHT ON HIS OWN FEET . HE WILL BE TAUGHT REVERENCE FOR HIS OWN SPIRIT.

WHEN I SHALL HAVE READ ALL THE BOOKS, AND LEARNED MY NEW WAY...WHEN MY HOME WILL BE READY, AND MY EARTH TILLED...
I SHALL STEAL AWAY ONE DAY... FOR ONE LAST TIME--INTO THE CURSED CITY OF MY BIRTH.
I SHALL CALL TO ME MY FRIEND WHO HAS NO NAME, SAVE INTERNATIONAL 4-8818.
...AND ALL THOSE LIKE HIM--
FRATERNITY 2-5503...WHO CRIES FOR NO REASON, AND SOLIDARITY 9-6347... WHO CALLS FOR HELP IN THE NIGHT-- AND A FEW OTHERS.
I SHALL CALL TO ME ALL OF THE MEN AND WOMEN WHOSE SPIRIT HAS NOT BEEN KILLED WITHIN THEM... AND WHO SUFFER UNDER THE YOKE OF THEIR BROTHERS.
THEY WILL FOLLOW ME, AND I SHALL LEAD THEM TO MY FORTRESS.
AND HERE-- IN THIS UNCHARTED WILDERNESS...I AND THEY--MY CHOSEN FRIENDS, MY FELLOW BUILDERS, SHALL WRITE THE FIRST CHAPTER IN THE NEW HISTORY OF MAN.

THESE ARE THE THINGS BEFORE ME...
I LOOK BEHIND ME FOR THE LAST TIME...
I LOOK UPON THE HISTORY OF MEN...WHICH I HAVE LEARNED FROM THE BOOKS--AND I WONDER...
IT WAS A LONG STORY...AND THE SPIRIT WHICH MOVED IT WAS THE SPIRIT OF MAN'S FREEDOM.
BUT WHAT IS FREEDOM?!
IN CONGRESS, JULY 4, 1776.
A DECLARATION
BY THE REPRESENTATIVES OF THE
UNITED STATES OF AMERICA,
IN GENERAL CONGRESS ASSEMBLED.
THERE IS NOTHING TO TAKE A MAN'S FREEDOM AWAY FROM HIM... SAVE OTHER MEN.
TO BE FREE A MAN MUST BE FREE OF HIS BROTHERS.
THAT IS FREEDOM.
THAT AND NOTHING ELSE.

AT FIRST... MAN WAS ENSLAVED BY THE GODS...
BUT HE BROKE THEIR CHAINS...
THEN HE WAS ENSLAVED BY THE KINGS...
BUT HE BROKE THEIR CHAINS.
HE WAS ENSLAVED BY HIS BIRTH...BY HIS KIN-- BY HIS RACE...
BUT HE BROKE THEIR CHAINS.
HE DECLARED TO ALL HIS BROTHERS THAT A MAN HAS RIGHTS WHICH NEITHER GOD, NOR KING ...NOR OTHER MEN CAN TAKE AWAY FROM HIM...
...FOR THIS IS THE RIGHT OF MAN... AND THERE IS NO RIGHT ON EARTH ABOVE THIS RIGHT.
...AND HE STOOD ON THE THRESHOLD OF THE FREEDOM FOR WHICH BLOOD OF THE CENTURIES HAD BEEN SPILLED.

BUT THEN HE GAVE UP ALL HE HAD ...AND FELL LOWER THAN HIS SAVAGE BEGINNING.
WHAT BROUGHT IT TO PASS?! WHAT DISASTER TOOK THEIR REASON AWAY FROM MEN?!
WHAT WHIP LASHED THEM TO THEIR KNEES IN SHAME AND SUBMISSION?!
...THE WORSHIP OF THE WORD "WE."
WHEN MEN ACCEPTED THAT WORSHIP...THE STRUCTURE OF CENTURIES COLLAPSED ABOUT THEM...
...THE STRUCTURE WHOSE EVERY BEAM HAD COME FROM THE THOUGHT OF SOME ONE MAN...
...EACH IN HIS DAY DOWN THE AGES FROM THE DEPTH OF SOME ONE SPIRIT--SUCH SPIRIT AS EXISTED FOR ITS OWN SAKE.
THOSE EAGER TO OBEY...EAGER TO LIVE FOR ONE ANOTHER...SINCE THEY HAD NOTHING TO VINDICATE THEM--THOSE MEN---COULD NEITHER CARRY ON...NOR PRESERVE WHAT THEY HAD RECEIVED.
THUS DID ALL THOUGHT...ALL SCIENCE...ALL WISDOM--PERISH ON EARTH.
THUS DID MEN--WITH NOTHING TO OFFER SAVE THEIR GREAT NUMBER--LOSE THE STEEL TOWERS, THE FLYING SHIPS, THE POWER WIRES... ALL THE THINGS THEY HAD NOT CREATED, AND COULD NEVER KEEP.
PERHAPS SOME MEN HAD BEEN BORN WITH THE MIND AND THE COURAGE TO RECOVER THESE THINGS WHICH WERE LOST. PERHAPS THEY CAME BEFORE THE COUNCIL OF SCHOLARS...
THEY WERE ANSWERED AS I HAVE BEEN---AND FOR THE SAME REASONS.

BUT STILL I WONDER HOW IT WAS POSSIBLE, IN THOSE GRACELESS YEARS OF TRANSITION... LONG AGO--THAT MEN DID NOT SEE WHITHER THEY WERE GOING, AND WENT ON...IN BLINDNESS, AND COWARDICE TO THEIR FATE.
I WONDER--FOR IT IS HARD FOR ME TO CONCEIVE HOW MEN WHO KNEW THE WORD "I" COULD GIVE IT UP AND NOT KNOW WHAT THEY LOST.
BUT SUCH HAS BEEN THE STORY...FOR I HAVE LIVED IN THE CITY OF THE DAMNED.
...AND I KNOW WHAT HORROR MEN PERMITTED TO BE BROUGHT UPON THEM.
HERETIC

PERHAPS...IN THOSE DAYS...THERE WERE A FEW AMONG MEN... A FEW OF CLEAR SIGHT AND CLEAN SOUL--WHO REFUSED TO SURRENDER THAT WORD...
WHAT AGONY MUST HAVE BEEN THEIRS-- BEFORE THAT WHICH THEY SAW COMING, AND COULD NOT STOP IT...

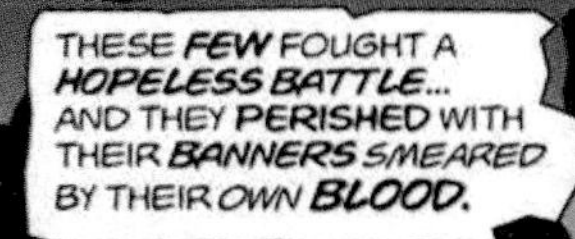
THESE FEW FOUGHT A HOPELESS BATTLE... AND THEY PERISHED WITH THEIR BANNERS SMEARED BY THEIR OWN BLOOD.
AND THEY CHOSE TO PERISH...FOR THEY KNEW. TO THEM I SEND MY SALUTE ACROSS THE CENTURIES-- AND MY PITY.

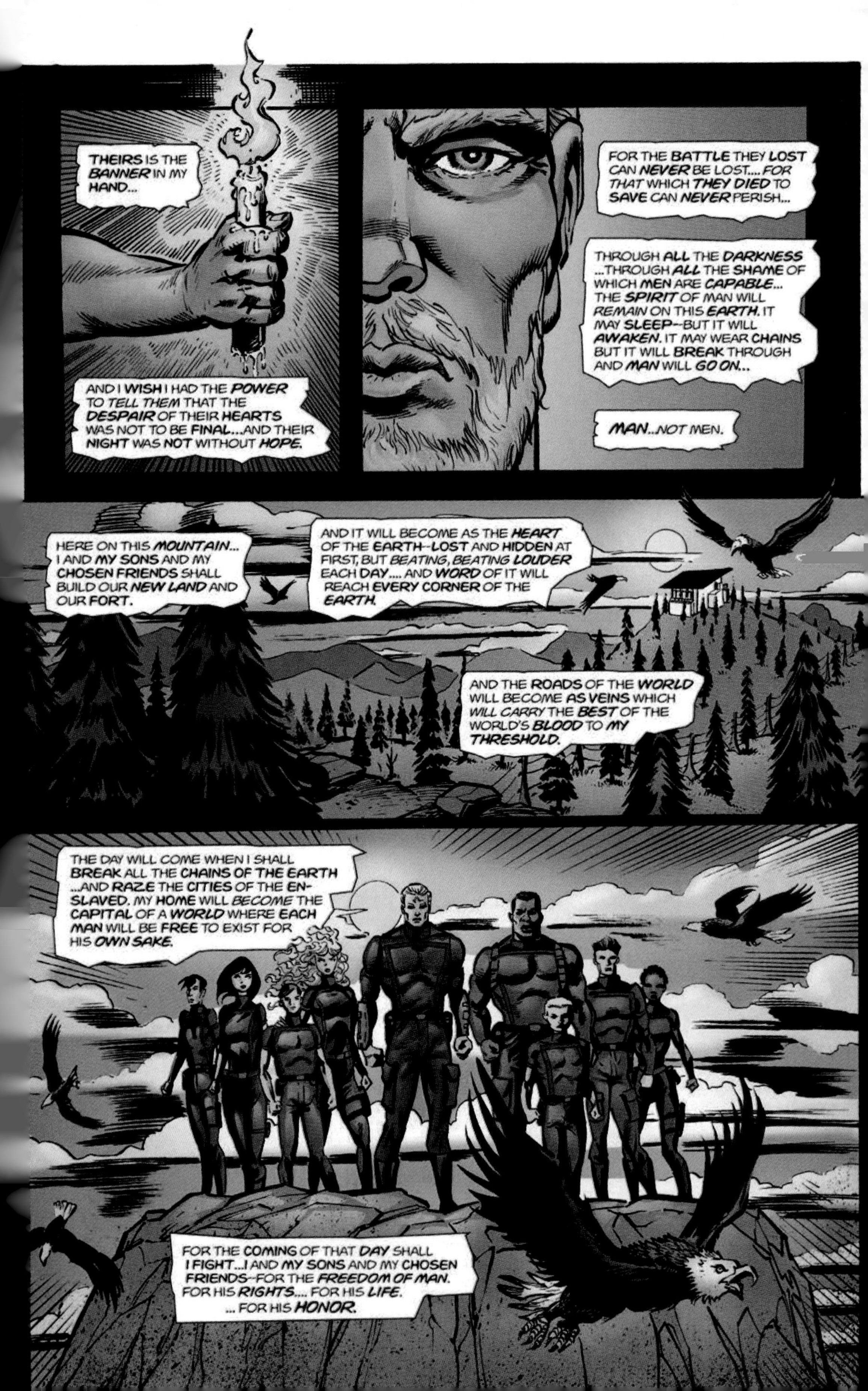
THEIRS IS THE BANNER IN MY HAND...
AND I WISH I HAD THE POWER TO TELL THEM THAT THE DESPAIR OF THEIR HEARTS WAS NOT TO BE FINAL...AND THEIR NIGHT WAS NOT WITHOUT HOPE.
FOR THE BATTLE THEY LOST CAN NEVER BE LOST.... FOR THAT WHICH THEY DIED TO SAVE CAN NEVER PERISH...
THROUGH ALL THE DARKNESS ...THROUGH ALL THE SHAME OF WHICH MEN ARE CAPABLE... THE SPIRIT OF MAN WILL REMAIN ON THIS EARTH. IT MAY SLEEP--BUT IT WILL AWAKEN. IT MAY WEAR CHAINS BUT IT WILL BREAK THROUGH AND MAN WILL GO ON...
MAN...NOT MEN.
HERE ON THIS MOUNTAIN... I AND MY SONS AND MY CHOSEN FRIENDS SHALL BUILD OUR NEW LAND AND OUR FORT.
AND IT WILL BECOME AS THE HEART OF THE EARTH--LOST AND HIDDEN AT FIRST, BUT BEATING, BEATING LOUDER EACH DAY.... AND WORD OF IT WILL REACH EVERY CORNER OF THE EARTH.
AND THE ROADS OF THE WORLD WILL BECOME AS VEINS WHICH WILL CARRY THE BEST OF THE WORLD'S BLOOD TO MY THRESHOLD.
THE DAY WILL COME WHEN I SHALL BREAK ALL THE CHAINS OF THE EARTH ...AND RAZE THE CITIES OF THE EN-SLAVED. MY HOME WILL BECOME THE CAPITAL OF A WORLD WHERE EACH MAN WILL BE FREE TO EXIST FOR HIS OWN SAKE.
FOR THE COMING OF THAT DAY SHALL I FIGHT...I AND MY SONS AND MY CHOSEN FRIENDS--FOR THE FREEDOM OF MAN. FOR HIS RIGHTS.... FOR HIS LIFE. ... FOR HIS HONOR.

FOR THE FREEDOM OF MAN...
FOR HIS RIGHTS...
FOR HIS LIFE...
FOR HIS HONOR.
AND HERE OVER THE PORTALS OF MY FORT... I SHALL CUT THE WORD WHICH IS TO BE MY BEACON, AND MY BANNER...
THE WORD WHICH WILL NOT DIE...SHOULD WE ALL PERISH IN BATTLE...
EGO
THE WORD WHICH CAN NEVER DIE ON THIS EARTH...
FOR IT IS THE HEART OF IT... AND THE MEANING...
...AND THE GLORY.
1984 George Orwell
FOUNTAIN HEAD RAND
ANTHEM AYN RAND
Atlas Shrugged AYN RAND
BRAVE NEW WORLD HUXLEY
finis

About The Atlas Society

The Atlas Society is a non-profit educational organization advancing the ideals of reason, achievement, benevolence and ethical self-interest as the moral foundations for political liberty, personal happiness and a flourishing society. The thirty year-old philosophy think tank builds on **Ayn Rand's** works and ideas, using artistic and other creative means to reach and inspire new audiences.

In addition to our publications — including the popular ***Pocket Guide to Objectivism*** — our viral videos, distributed via social media, range from comedic live action to music videos to *Draw My Life* features. **Educational Resources** include online courses, live webinars, campus speaking tours, weekend retreats, living history presentations and various campus activism projects.

To learn more visit our website — **atlassociety.org** — or find us on *Facebook*, *Twitter* or *Instagram*.

First Printing 2016

ISBN: 978-1-7326037-0-7
PCN: 2018953532

The Atlas Society Press
800 Rockmead Drive, #200
Kingwood, TX 77339
www.atlassociety.org